T0329246

THE ECONOMICS OF
BUSINESS LIFE

THE ECONOMICS OF BUSINESS LIFE

by

SIR HENRY PENSON
K.B.E., M.A.

*formerly Lecturer in Economics in the
University of Oxford*

Author of "The Economics of Everyday Life"

CAMBRIDGE
AT THE UNIVERSITY PRESS
1933

CAMBRIDGE
UNIVERSITY PRESS

University Printing House, Cambridge CB2 8BS, United Kingdom

Cambridge University Press is part of the University of Cambridge.

It furthers the University's mission by disseminating knowledge in the pursuit of education, learning and research at the highest international levels of excellence.

www.cambridge.org
Information on this title: www.cambridge.org/9781107586604

© Cambridge University Press 1933

First published 1933
First paperback edition 2015

A catalogue record for this publication is available from the British Library

ISBN 978-1-107-58660-4 Paperback

PREFACE

Some people may be inclined to doubt whether any useful purpose is served by attempting to introduce Economics into the matter-of-fact conditions of ordinary business life. They may urge that a study of Economics is all very well for the student, but that it would be better for the business man to concentrate on learning his job and mastering the rules of success. Economics, it is true, does not pretend to teach people how to learn a business, or how to become successful business men, but it does teach something of the forces which underlie all economic activity, and business is merely the form which economic activity takes, the method by which economic wants can have their fulfilment. Hence these two points of view, the theoretical and the practical, may well be considered in their relation to one another, a study of business life bringing reality into the study of economics, and the study of economics bringing clearness and grasp into that of business life.

The object of the present work is twofold:

(1) to present a kind of economic background for a picture of business life, and

(2) to fill in the details of the picture by describing something of the machinery by which that business life is carried on.

Hence the division of the book into two parts:

Part I. The Economic Side of Life.

Part II. Business Life and Institutions.

The Economics of Business Life may be regarded to some extent as complementary to the author's earlier work *The Economics of Everyday Life*, for whereas the latter was concerned with the fundamental causes of economic activity and with the working of economic forces generally, the former, as its title suggests, is more concerned with the actualities of economic life, with the methods which have been devised and with the institutions which have been set up to secure its smooth and efficient working. Thus it is more practical and at the same time more advanced, for it has in view the needs of those who may be taking up business life as a career as well as of those who merely wish to get some clearer idea as to the general conduct of business affairs. It is neither a textbook of economics nor a manual of business practice, but it should serve as an introduction to the more detailed study of both.

Throughout the book an attempt is made to connect the present with the past, in pursuance of which plan short historical introductions are given with the object of showing how the various business institutions came to take their present form.

The arrangement by which each chapter has been made as self-contained as possible has involved a certain amount of repetition, which could only have been avoided by constantly referring the reader to what had been said before, a very irritating practice. This applies more particularly to the chapters on Banking, the Gold Standard, and International Trade, in all of which, for example, it was impossible to avoid some reference to such questions as Currency and Bills of Exchange.

T.H.P.

September 1933

CONTENTS

PART I

THE ECONOMIC SIDE OF LIFE

PART II

BUSINESS LIFE AND INSTITUTIONS

PART I

THE ECONOMIC SIDE OF LIFE

CHAPTER I

THE ORDINARY BUSINESS OF LIFE

ECONOMICS DEFINED

The late Professor Marshall of Cambridge defined Economics as being "the study of mankind in the ordinary business of life".[1] Described in this way it would seem as if the subject ought to present very little difficulty even to a beginner, inasmuch as it deals with something with which all people are more or less familiar. Perhaps it is the word ordinary which gives us this impression, but the simplicity is more apparent than real, for when we come to look into it more closely it soon becomes evident that the business of life is in reality a very complicated thing, so complicated in fact that even an elementary understanding of its working cannot be acquired without quite a considerable amount of investigation and study.

The word "business", as it is generally used, implies a good deal more than mere occupation or activity: it means activity in certain very definite directions. From the economic point of view the great preoccupation of most individuals is how to obtain an income, for it is in that way alone that they can arrive at that which is the ultimate end and object of all economic activity, viz. the satisfaction of their daily wants. Hence the getting of an income and the using of it for the satisfaction of wants may be regarded at this early stage of the discussion as a very brief, yet sufficiently accurate statement of what is meant by "the ordinary business of life".

---

[1] Marshall, *Principles of Economics*, Book I, Chap. I.

INCOME AND SERVICE

Income is obtained as a return for economic service rendered and economic service takes a variety of forms: it may be personal service, or it may be the service of property. It is usual to differentiate between two kinds of personal service, viz. the service of hand and the service of brain, but this classification is not very exact or complete, for many forms of service, that of the skilled artisan for example, demand both physical and mental effort. The distinction, however, is in general sufficiently clear, and when we speak of manual workers and brain workers there is no confusion in our minds as to the type of work each is doing. Suffice it to say that the term personal service includes every kind of effort, whether of the organizer, the manager, or the inventor, of the artisan in the workshop or the clerk in the office, of doctors, lawyers, schoolmasters, and other professional men, of all who contribute to the supply of what we consume, or minister to our comfort, convenience, amusement, or happiness.

The services of property are perhaps not quite so obvious, but they play a necessary part in the economic effort and consequently they receive in the form of income a share of the wealth produced. For example, a person may own land, which he does not wish to cultivate himself and he therefore lets it to a farmer, who pays him rent for it. The farmer may need more stock, more implements, more fertilizers than his own capital resources can provide. He therefore borrows, let us say from the Bank, the additional capital he needs and pays interest on it. Those who supply him with land and capital are rendering him services for which he pays out a portion of the product of the farm. Rent therefore in the one case and interest in the other may be considered as forms of income, derived from the services of these two kinds of property, land and capital.

The relation between Income and Service may be regarded as the mainspring of our economic life, for economic life is in essence the exchange, or rather the interchange, of service, and, since income is the return for economic service while income in its turn brings the satisfaction of our wants, it is clear that income and service are inextricably bound up together. In this way we all become economically interdependent, a point of view which will be dealt with more fully later on.

Income can be regarded from three points of view: that of the individual, that of the industrial group of which he is a member, and that of the community to which he belongs. This last may be termed the National Income, for it is not only the sum total of the economic services rendered by the people of a country during a given period, for example a year, or in other words what the nation has produced during that period, but it is also the sum total of the individual incomes of all the people of the country. Some incomes it would be readily understood must not be reckoned in this total, for they are mere transfers of income from one person to another without the rendering of economic service in exchange. The allowance which a father makes to his son is a good example of this, for the spending power of the one is diminished by what is added to the spending power of the other. Income, then, may be considered as equivalent to Spending Power.

If the individual citizen is a member of an industrial group his or her income is a part of the income of that group and varies with the nature and amount of the service rendered. Services are not all alike and incomes also may differ widely from one another. This gives rise to the most difficult of all economic problems, the problem of distribution, as it is called. Many have taken part in the productive act: what is to be the particular share of each? This question may be answered very shortly as follows: "According to the valuation which society puts upon each particular form of service". If society, that

is people in general, desires something very much and it is
very scarce or otherwise very difficult to obtain, a higher price
will be paid for it than would be paid for a thing the desire
for which is less strong or the supply of it more easily come
by. What is true of commodities is true also of services, and
this provides an explanation why the income of a prima donna
is higher than that of a member of the chorus, or the income
of the business organizer higher than that of one of the clerks
in the office.

Some people find it difficult to understand that this in-
equality in individual incomes is not a purely arbitrary thing.
They fail to see in it the result of the interaction of those
economic forces usually spoken of as Supply and Demand.
Salaries and wages are in general determined by circumstances
over which the employer has very little control. There is
besides no fixed standard of measurement which can be applied to all the different types of service such as there is for
length or weight. Time, intensity of effort, skill have all something to do with the measurement, but there are other factors
as well, the two chief of which are the ability which the product has to satisfy the public want and the ease or difficulty
with which persons can be found with the necessary qualifications for the duties required of them.

Under modern conditions income is measured in terms of
money and takes the form of money. There is some difference
in meaning, however, between these two uses of the term
money. In the first case by money is meant the standard unit
of currency in the country, that is pounds sterling in Great
Britain, dollars in the U.S.A., marks in Germany, francs in
France. In the second case the term money is used to cover
the accepted medium of exchange. It may be coin or bank-
notes, both of which are money in the technical sense, but it
may also be that which gives one the right to receive money,
for example, a cheque or a bill of exchange; in fact, money
in this wider sense may be said to include everything that has

general purchasing power, everything through which exchanges can be effected, by means of which wants both
material and immaterial can be satisfied. Thus the getting of
a money income is not an end in itself, it is merely the means
to an end, and income is valued only for what it will bring.
How much a given income will bring depends on the general
level of prices, and on these two factors—money income and
price level—depends what is called the Standard of Living.

EARNING AND SPENDING

The getting of an income, and the using of it for the satisfaction of wants, involves two sets of economic or, to use a
less technical term, business relations: those which are connected on the one hand with earning the income, and on the
other with the spending of it. With many persons, especially
those whose incomes are small, fairly regular, and fixed in
amount, both of these relations tend to become mere matters
of habit and routine. As regards the earning, one day is for
them very much the same as another: a fixed number of
hours' work each day; the same type of work, perhaps, and
a more or less fixed amount of it to be got through in the day,
and always in the same office or workshop. In return for this
economic effort income is received at regular intervals in the
form of wages or salary, and these, too, may vary very little
from month to month and from year to year. As regards the
spending, the income is applied to the maintenance of a
standard of life which for some time perhaps has become so
established that everything connected with it has become
almost automatic, almost mechanical. One portion of the
income week by week, or month by month, is assigned to
rent, another to general household expenses, a third to clothing, a fourth perhaps to school fees, and, according as the
income permits of it, to some provision for entertainment,
holidays, a motor car, doctors' bills, etc. Thrift, too, may
enter into the calculations of the more prudent, or the more

ambitious—and a sum, larger or smaller as the case may be, is set aside regularly by way of savings. By some this will be regarded as a provision for the rainy day, or for old age; by others as a means of getting on and of becoming more independent; of raising the standard of living and of improving the economic position generally.

THE WIDER VIEW

With many, no doubt, owing to narrowness of circumstances and outlook, such a condition of things as has just been described, the monotony of which is only broken by occasional periods of sickness or unemployment or perhaps changes in rates of wages or salaries, has come to be regarded as the ordinary business of life. Such people are in the main either ignorant of or indifferent to that wider economic life, which is the concern of the community as a whole, and which is often beyond their very limited horizon. The daily work and what it will bring is to them not unnaturally the all-important matter. But without losing sight of the significance to each individual of his or her immediate and personal interest, we have to remember that all are affected by general business conditions and, consequently, when we are dealing with the business of life we must take into consideration the general aspects of that economic activity which is going on in the world outside us. Our subject embraces something even more than the relations between employers and employed on the one hand, and of buyers and sellers on the other, more also than negotiations as to the terms of payment for services rendered, and negotiations as to the price of goods offered for sale. Behind these apparently simple forms of economic relationship—though these are not by any means so simple as they appear—there lies something far more complicated and difficult to understand, something of which, owing to the fact perhaps that our personal contact with it is so much on the surface, we may even fail to realize the existence. This is business in the larger sense of the term: business as it is understood, not in the household but in the great city: business from the point of view of that somewhat indefinite body, the business world.

ECONOMIC LIFE

The business world, however, is apt to be more concerned with the daily operations of business life and with those actions of individuals or governments which tend to assist or to hamper its smooth working than with the principles which underlie the economic life of the community as a whole or of the world in general. But some clear understanding of economic life and of the forces at work in connection with it is absolutely essential to any intelligent grasp of business problems and of the working of business institutions, and hence the first part of this book is in the main devoted to a consideration of this subject.

In the first place we must guard against taking too narrow a view of this economic life, that is to say, we must not think of it merely as something which affects ourselves only. Nor must we take too short a view and concentrate on the immediate results of any particular course of action without due regard to what may happen in the future. Moreover, it is necessary at all times to bear in mind how closely bound up together, economically speaking, we all are. There is no individual who does not play some part in the economic life of the community of which he or she is a member and who is not affected therefore in greater or lesser degree by the actions of others.

In the everyday economic life we seem to be up against a continual conflict of interests, each individual wanting to get as much as possible in the way of income for the services he renders and to give as little as possible out of that income for the services which others render to him. But in our anxiety to buy as cheaply as possible we are apt to lose sight of the fact that the price of the article has to remunerate quite a number of services of different kinds, and that if this price is less than what will afford a reasonable return for all these services, some at any rate of those who have rendered them will suffer a loss which will ultimately react on the buyers themselves.

At a time when the general price level is low money goes much farther in satisfying the household needs than it does at a time when the level is high. At first sight this would seem to be a very great advantage, and to those with a fixed income there is no doubt that it would in reality be so. But these are only the comparatively few; the majority of incomes are dependent upon general prosperity and this in its turn on business being conducted with a margin of profit. The low prices appear to be good for the housewife, though they may inflict injury on the breadwinner whose income may have fallen in consequence of them, and who may even have become temporarily unemployed. Taking society as a whole, housewives and breadwinners, consumers and producers, have not really two separate interests, they are merely two aspects of the economic life of the household. The housewife can only spend what the breadwinner has earned, and what the one may have gained as a consumer the other may have more than lost as a producer.

The great English statesman, William Huskisson, when speaking in the House of Commons in 1815, a few months before the close of the Napoleonic Wars, uttered these very striking words:

Nothing can be more fallacious than the notion that cheapness in the price of provisions is always of benefit. Cheapness without the demand for labour is a symptom of distress; cheapness always prevails where enterprise is at a stand. The great object to be attained is steady prices and an active demand for labour.

The same thing has recently been said, though in other words, by some of the great financial experts of the day, and it is not infrequently asserted, and the opinion is supported by some of the highest authorities, that the low price level of commodities is the real cause of the present[1] world-wide depression. Prices have fallen below a remunerative figure, demand for labour has decreased, and incomes are smaller all round. There is, consequently, less demand for commodities and this causes prices to fall still further. Thus we get into a vicious circle, poverty creating still greater poverty.

Every economic change, although it may appear only to affect the lives of a very few, has in reality a far wider effect than can be seen or traced. Some piece of labour-saving machinery, for example, is introduced with the immediate consequence no doubt that certain persons lose their employment and that others gain by the cheapening of the process or by a reduction in the price of the particular article. But in the long run the effect may prove to be a much greater demand for the product, and ultimately some increase in the total number of persons employed in its manufacture as well as an increase in the general demand for other kinds of labour owing to the increase in purchasing power of those immediately affected.

An economic change is like the throwing of a stone into a pond. The immediate result is a splash which directs attention to a particular spot, but the disturbance does not end there: the ripples on the water will widen and widen until they reach the extreme circumference of the pond, and it is seen that all the water in some degree has been affected by the casting of that stone.

THE ECONOMIC DAY

With the great majority of people the economic day begins with "going to business", for nowadays the daily bread is seldom earned in the home, but rather in the factory, the workshop, or the office. Those working in large cities must

[1] Written in 1933.

often live at a distance from their place of business, and hence in the early morning one may see every weekday streams of people, of all ages and all ranks of society, pouring into one of the great industrial or commercial centres, having come by train or tram, by bus or car as the case may be. It is the beginning of the economic day, the first and necessary stage of each day's activity.

The hurrying crowd consists of all sorts and conditions of men and women. Some are employers of labour, some are employed, some are connected with large businesses and some with small, some are occupying positions of great responsibility and some have merely to follow out the instructions of those above them. However different their circumstances may be, they are all animated by the same motive, they have all a common aim, viz. that which has already been set out as the object of all economic activity, the satisfaction of the daily wants. Each is occupied doubtless with his or her own personal interests, occupations and circumstances, and such thought as is given to the day's work which is lying ahead is probably devoted to the individual part which he or she has to play rather than to the problems of business in general. With most of them, doubtless, the horizon is to a large extent limited by the home from which they have come and the particular business or occupation to which they are going. How many of them realize that the interests of all the various human elements in that thronging mass of people are in some way or other closely interrelated, or that all are, to some extent, dependent on one another; that all are taking part in a great combination of effort on the collective result of which depends the economic welfare of the society to which they belong? Yet this is what it really amounts to, for each is contributing something to that vast sum total of economic services which provides food, clothing and shelter, necessaries, comforts and luxuries, for the community as a whole.

To each, as has already been pointed out, the particular form of work is merely à means to an end. The end is the satisfaction of personal or family needs. The means is the weekly wage, the monthly salary, the fees or commissions, the business profits, or whatever form the income may take. Here we have the very foundation of our economic life. It originates with human needs, to satisfy which there must be economic effort. Everyone is a consumer, but effort, or, to use the more technical term, production, must precede the satisfaction of wants, that is to say consumption. In a modern society each consumes what others produce and this involves giving something in exchange. That something is a part of the money income resulting from one's own contribution of effort which has served to meet the needs of someone else. Hence it is clear that to satisfy one's own wants one must first satisfy the wants of other people. If a person is unemployed, that is, if he ceases for the time being to render any economic service, the income which is the reward for that service also ceases and with it the ability or the power to demand the services of others, unless he has provided for such a contingency either by having saved when he was in a position to do so or by having contributed to some form of insurance or pension scheme. If his spending power is increased beyond these limits it is either by the voluntary or compulsory contribution of other people, but this is merely a transfer of income from one person to another and does not affect the general economic principle enunciated above, that one must render some service that will satisfy the wants of others, before one can be in a position to satisfy one's own.

Reference has already been made to the two kinds of service, the personal service of hand or brain and the service of property, and what has just been said about the unemployment of labour is quite as true about the unemployment of capital, for if capital is lying idle the income that would have been derived from the service it was able to render also ceases and the spending power of the owners of the unemployed capital is consequently reduced.

It must, however, always be borne in mind that the service of capital can only be rendered in conjunction with labour. Without labour capital would be sterile; without capital labour would be unproductive; and hence unemployment as usually understood is always accompanied by the unemployment—or underemployment—of capital. Thus the national income suffers a double loss, loss of wages or salaries on the one hand and loss of profits on the other.

ECONOMIC INTERDEPENDENCE

This leads us on to consider rather more closely the interdependence of all the various sections of our economic society. The falling off in general purchasing power shows itself first in the decrease of retail trade. If the tradesman does not sell his goods, he can place fewer orders with those who supply him, and if they are middlemen they in their turn can place fewer orders with growers and manufacturers. As a result traders, middlemen, growers and manufacturers all have reduced incomes. They spend less and the vicious circle comes round again, bringing with it still more unemployment of both labour and capital. Hence just as it is true to say that "labour is the demand for labour" so is the contrary equally true that "unemployment breeds unemployment", and trade depression leads to still greater depression until, unless counteracted in time, a crisis results.

When, on the other hand, the tide turns and business begins to improve, the same interdependence of the various sections of economic society manifests itself. The increasing confidence which leads to bigger orders and better prices for manufacturers and growers results in a greater demand for labour, in higher wages, in greater profits and in increased spending power all round, which in its turn helps to speed up the general improvement.

It is only natural that each individual in that hurrying crowd described above as "going to business" should think chiefly of how the day's work is likely to affect him or her economically, for a loss of situation to one would bring anxiety and hardship to the home while to another an unsuccessful business venture might result in closing down the undertaking altogether and might jeopardize seriously his own chances of livelihood as well as those of the various members of his staff. Or, if it happened to be the other way round, and the day brought with it an increase of salary to one, or the securing of some large order or contract to another, it would result in a measure of increased economic satisfaction for the person immediately concerned. But in no case, it may safely be said, would the loss or the gain affect the individual alone, for what affects one concerns all.

In conclusion, this idea of economic interdependence can be summed up in the simple statement that no one can live economically unto himself or herself. What affects the life of one is bound to affect also the lives of many others, and as with individuals so with nations. No nation can live economically unto itself. Its conditions of production and of sale, its financial stability and the policy of its Government will affect the lives and happiness of people all over the world.

CHAPTER II

THE ECONOMIC MACHINE

In the preceding chapter attention was concentrated on some of the more general features of our economic life; in the present one the subject will be carried somewhat further by looking more closely at its method of working.

For this purpose it will be convenient to treat economic life as being in some respects comparable to an elaborate piece of machinery, and there is some justification for such a procedure, inasmuch as there is in both a similar complexity of construction and a similar interdependence of the various parts. The analogy must not of course be carried too far, but it may well serve to illustrate some very valuable economic truths, and above all it will help to keep before our minds the importance of regarding the community as being one economic whole and not so much as consisting of individuals or classes with separate or even opposing interests.

Before proceeding to examine all that is implied in this conception of an economic machine, it may be well to set out very briefly some of the more striking points of resemblance between our economic life and a mechanical contrivance of this kind.

(1) In both there seems to be some kind of compelling force which keeps everything in motion.

(2) Both consist of many separate parts but all of them fit in together, all are dependent upon one another. Detached from one another the parts would cease to have any meaning or purpose. All members of a society are parts of the body economic, and like the parts of a machine each individual must fit into his or her own particular place, and each must discharge his or her own particular function.

(3) In both there is a definite end or purpose towards which all the operations are directed and for which the whole structure has been designed.

There is, however, an important consideration which must not be lost sight of, and it is this: though our economic life may be regarded in some respects as resembling the working of a machine, it is not something mechanical, for a society consists of individuals who can and do act independently of one another. All are not influenced by the same motives, some being more calculating than others, some more altruistic, some more emotional. Moreover, by the exercise of will-power the individual is able to help or to hinder the smooth working of the economic machine or even to put it out of action altogether.

Our study of the economic machine can conveniently be arranged under the following three headings:

(1) The Purpose.
(2) The Working.
(3) The Control.

(1) THE PURPOSE

What is the object or purpose of the economic machine? The answer can be given very shortly. It is for the more complete satisfaction of human wants or, in other words, for economic well-being. When we consider how very intricate the processes of economic life really are, when we picture to ourselves the distance in time and space that separates producer and consumer, we can see that before human wants can be satisfied there is a great gap to be bridged and it is the bridging of that gap, the adjusting of supply to demand, of human effort to human needs, that is the object or purpose of the economic machine. How this gap has arisen and how it has gradually become wider and wider can only be seen if we review something of the economic history of the past few centuries, but it is essential to our subject that this should be clearly understood, and hence in the next chapter a brief survey will be given of the development of economic life, showing how that life has from great simplicity become more and more complex, and how the self-sufficiency of earlier times has given place to mutual interdependence.

(2) THE WORKING

When trying to understand and to follow the working of the economic machine we are confronted with a very great difficulty, and this arises from that extreme complexity which, as already pointed out, is one of the outstanding characteristics of modern economic life.

Anyone not technically efficient would experience precisely the same difficulty with regard to any piece of complicated machinery. The ordinary traveller on board a steamship, for example, might chance to look down from above into the engine room. What impression would he get? He would see before him a vast combination of rods and wheels, of cranks, pistons and belts. He would get the idea that all of those various parts are in some way connected with one another, but in exactly what way he would not have the slightest conception.

He could well imagine that there must be some source of power that sets everything in motion and that the result of all the activity and the noise is the revolution of the screw propeller which drives the ship forward. But he would not be able to see how the power is applied or what agency is contributing to the working of the whole machine. Yet, if the engineer were to act as an instructor and guide, that onlooker might easily get some clearer idea of what is going on. The plan and purpose of the machinery would become clearer to him when the essential features were pointed out and simply explained.

It is the same with our economic life. Regarding it from the outside, all that the mere onlooker could see would be a

very large number of human beings each, apparently, per-
forming some particular and independent function. He
would realize that the various forms of individual activity
must be in some way related to one another, and he might
grasp the fact that a certain number of those busily engaged
were co-operating in the production of some particular commodity, but he would probably fail to see how the various
groups of workers were connected and how it was that, though
they might be scattered all over the world, the collective
result of all their efforts taken together would be the satisfaction of the economic needs of people everywhere. What he
would need is that someone like the engineer should come
along who would point out exactly the forces which are
brought into play by the action of individuals or of groups,
who would give him some idea of the links which bind the
various forms of activity together and of the connecting rods
which communicate motion and direction to the manifold
types of effort.

This need of guidance is well illustrated by the difficulty
often experienced in understanding both the causes of the
general trade depression which began in the latter part of
1929 and the arguments brought forward for and against the
various remedial measures proposed. All have recognized
that the economic machine is working badly, that some parts
of it look as if they might break down altogether and by so
doing still further interfere with its proper action. We are
often told that the real cause of the depression is the fall in
prices, that the low prices result from scarcity of currency and
that this in its turn arises from the immobilization of large
quantities of gold, but how and why this should be so seems
to require a good deal of explanation. By several experts,
again, we are told that the remedy is to be found in an increase
in the amount of the currency in circulation which would
involve an extension of general purchasing power. But most
people find it difficult to understand exactly how this will

bring about the desired effect, and they feel the need of some enlightenment from one of these experts making clear how the effect of such an operation will be transmitted from one part of the economic machine to another, until the working of the whole has been speeded up and improved.

The first thing to look into is the question of the motive power. What is it that starts the economic machine to work? The answer is a simple one, for that initial impulse comes from nothing more or less than human wants: wants which cannot be satisfied without some form of effort, the effort of oneself and the associated efforts of one's fellow men. In other words, the impulse to all economic activity comes from the desire to consume, that is, to obtain the satisfaction of one's wants. In a modern type of society wants are not satisfied by direct effort, that is, by the individual producing what he or she happens to want, but by producing the things that other people want. This brings us again to the idea of economic interdependence, to which attention has already been drawn.

In modern economic life, too, there is such an amount of what may be called auxiliary service. A large number of people may be engaged in a biscuit factory, but in addition to those actually engaged in the various processes connected with the making of biscuits many will be engaged in various other ways. Some, for example, will be employed in the office, keeping the books or making out invoices, while others will be doing secretarial work, writing letters, answering inquiries, and so on. Some may be merely running errands, or helping to transfer materials or finished products from one part of the works to another. Some, again, will be engaged in the engine room, others in the packing department, and so on almost indefinitely. Many hundreds of people are rendering one type of service or another, not all of them by any means actually making biscuits, yet all contributing in greater or less degree to the purpose for which the factory was established, namely, the supplying of biscuits to the consuming public. This example must be multiplied indefinitely before we can visualize in any way the immense amount of effort and the immense co-ordination of effort which is necessary before the wants of even the humblest individual can be satisfied.

But nothing has been said of other services which link together all these various types of effort and enable them to contribute to the satisfaction of the wants of the community. There must be transport, and banking, and insurance organizations, and within each of these again is a variety of effort, some of which is of a very highly skilled and responsible nature. The function of the banks is a particularly necessary one, for they provide what may be regarded as the lubrication of the economic machine. The various parts are brought into contact with one another through buying and selling, and buying and selling under modern conditions cannot go on without currency and credit, and the supply of these is the function of the banks.

When one realizes the complexity, the intricacy of this economic machine, it is not difficult to understand that it should often fail to work smoothly. Friction arises between the various parts. There may, on the one hand, be disputes between employers and employed, and on the other there may be a failure to adjust supply to demand, the result in both cases being the throwing of the economic machine out of gear and, as a consequence of this, an increase in the amount of unemployment.

(3) THE CONTROL

We have seen that the economic machine is started by human wants, and that it is lubricated by means of money and credit, but how is it regulated or controlled? The adjustment of supply to demand, which, as pointed out above, represents the purpose of the machine, is brought about through what is known as competition. It is, therefore, of very great importance to understand clearly what is meant by this term. As used in ordinary speech it hardly seems to need a definition. We are familiar with the idea in school work, in sport, in anything for which prizes are offered; and in the business world there is the competition between manufacturers to secure a market, between tradesmen to secure customers, and between those applying for any vacant post. But competition as the controlling force in economic life is an idea perhaps with which we are not so well acquainted.

COMPETITION

It has already been pointed out that economic life consists of the exchange of services, and the problem arises as to how much of one person's services must be given in exchange for those of others. What we may call the terms of the exchange is a matter of bargaining: each is demanding something that the other has and is supplying something that the other wants. There are certain conditions or forces affecting the demand, and there are certain conditions or forces affecting the supply. It is the interaction of these two forces, or sets of forces, which determines the terms of the exchange. When there is direct exchange between the two parties we speak of it as barter. When the exchange is indirect, that is, through the medium of a currency, we speak of it as sale and purchase and the terms of the exchange are spoken of as the price. The conditions of sale and purchase may be free, that is, left entirely to the individuals concerned, or they may be regulated by Guilds, by Trade Unions, by Local Authorities or by the State. Trade Unions are included in this statement because services may be exchanged as well as commodities, and rates of wages, which are virtually the price of services, emerge as the result of collective bargaining in which the Trade Union acts on behalf of all its members.

Arnold Toynbee, in his book on *The Industrial Revolution*

of the Eighteenth Century in England, says: "The essence of
the Industrial Revolution is the substitution of competition
for the mediaeval regulations which had previously controlled
production and distribution of wealth". This gives to competition the special meaning of freedom from restriction in
economic relations or, in other words, freedom for the forces
behind demand and behind supply to act and react upon one
another without interference of any kind, thus leaving the
terms of the exchange to be determined by the relative
economic strength of the two parties concerned. Adam Smith,
who wrote before the Industrial Revolution, regarded this
freedom in economic matters as the great ideal to which we
should strive to attain. His successors, Ricardo and Mill,
accepted it as the natural order of things, and it was on the
basis of free or perfect competition that they founded their
theories of value, of wages, of profits and of rent. These advocates of the doctrine of Natural Liberty contended that
competition, using the term to mean the complete absence of
external restraint in matters economic, could not fail to
secure the best interests of the community, the greatest
aggregate amount of wealth, the normal, or as they called it,
the natural price of commodities and the just remuneration
of both capital and labour. But the social evils which accompanied the Industrial Revolution were sufficient evidence
that absolutely unrestricted competition was not good for the
community as a whole, whatever benefits it might have
brought to individuals, and hence legislation of various kinds
has been passed throughout the past hundred years, not with
the object of doing away with competition, but of restricting
it in such a way as to protect the interests of those less able to
look after themselves. In saying, therefore, that the controlling force which regulates the working of the economic
machine is competition, we must understand that competition
to-day is restricted by many Acts of Parliament, limiting
hours of work, legalizing trade union action, introducing a

compulsory system of sickness and unemployment insurance, and more recently by Customs Tariffs for safeguarding or protecting particular industries and for giving preferential treatment in our markets to the products of the various parts of the British Empire. In many other matters, too numerous to mention, the State has intervened in the interests of the community at large, and by such intervention has imposed a restraint on the free exchange of goods as well as of services.

In spite of these limitations on individual freedom of action imposed by public authority, we may say that the individual is very largely free to pursue what he thinks to be his economic interest in the best way he can. He can choose his own occupation, he can buy and sell what he likes and make the best terms he can in his bargains.

Competition, then, resolves itself really into every individual pursuing his or her own interest with a view to securing the best economic results. How that interest can be best secured can only be the outcome of experience, and hence it may be said that self-interest guided by experience is the real controlling force regulating and directing the working of the economic machine. But here again we have an element of weakness. All do not know the direction in which their best economic interests really lie. Many mistakes, for example, are made in the choice of an occupation or profession. A boy may be led to take up a career for which he has no special aptitude or qualifications, or which may already be over-crowded, because at the time when he is entering upon the business of life it is not sufficiently clear for what calling he is best fitted, or where there is most room. Or even if he has a definite bent in some particular direction, for financial or other reasons he may not be able to follow it. In this way we get many square pegs in round holes and much economic waste is the result. Take, again, the case of a manufacturer who may be led to produce goods for which there is not a sufficient demand. His failure to judge the requirements of the market will again result in economic waste. Hence this policy of leaving each to do as he or she thinks best in his or her own interest may lead to much irregular working of the economic machine and to many instances of failure and disappointment.

ANTICIPATION

There is, however, another controlling force which is often responsible for the imperfect working of the economic machine and occasionally even for its partial breakdown. This we may describe as "anticipation". It is sometimes known as "speculation", but that is using the term in a strictly economic sense and not in that in which it is ordinarily employed. Speculation, economically speaking, simply means production of wealth in anticipation of a demand which may or may not be forthcoming, or, in the case of a merchant, buying on the prospect of selling at a profitable price. It would be difficult to imagine a state of things in which such anticipation played no part. Let us consider for a moment where we should be without it. When, for example, one goes to a tailor for a suit of clothes, one expects to be provided with a varied assortment of cloth. In anticipation of possible orders the tailor has had to get this stock of cloth in advance, but he could not have obtained it unless wool had been spun and woven into cloth some time before his order was received, and unless at a much earlier date still sheep-farmers, say in Australia, had produced the raw wool and shipped it to England for sale to the wool-spinning mills of Yorkshire. From this example it is clear that but for the enterprise of those who, recognizing that there was likely to be a market for what they produced, had expended labour and capital, time and thought and money, in anticipation of a possible demand for their products, it would not be possible to satisfy any but the simplest of our daily wants, at a time when and in the place where we might require to do so.

In many instances, more especially in the case of what are called primary products, that is, food and raw materials, it is absolutely necessary that the earlier processes of production should be taken in hand long before the product will be actually brought to market, and hence, expenses may be incurred which may not be covered by the price actually obtained. Taking wheat, for example, the farmer may judge from the prices of wheat prevailing, say in 1932, that it is in his interest to use certain portions of his land for wheat cultivation, and he ploughs and sows with the anticipation that in 1933 when his wheat is harvested it will fetch a remunerative price, but if the market has in the meantime fallen and the wheat in consequence is actually sold at a price lower than its cost of production, he will suffer considerable loss.

Or take an example of raw material, say rubber. The rubber has to be planted some years before it is actually put on the market, and hence this interval between planting and marketing renders accurate forecast practically impossible. Thus a kind of dislocation is liable to result, the effects of which may easily be felt to a greater or less degree throughout the whole of the body economic. Yet without such anticipation very few wants could be supplied and there could be no economic progress.

THE TWO SOLUTIONS

There are some who say that since the leaving of economic initiative and activity to individual decision and individual prospect of gain leads, and is in fact bound to lead, to economic dislocation and waste, and, as a consequence, to social hardship and distress, it is better to substitute for our individualistic system a system of State ownership of the means of production and of complete State regulation of economic life in general. There is a wide gulf between the two solutions of the economic problem, the individualistic and the socialistic, and it would be out of place in the present work to enter into any comparison of their respective merits. It must suffice merely to point out how immense the problem is, and how difficult it would be to set up an organization which could successfully co-ordinate the productive forces not merely of one country but of the whole world and be able to control the movements of the economic machine in such a way as to secure its smooth and accurate working. Any scheme of economic reorganization would need the most thorough and careful examination of its possible effect on the economic life of the community taken as a whole, not leaving out of sight the cardinal fact, to which reference has so frequently been made, that no individuals, no classes or groups, no nations, are economically independent of one another.

CHAPTER III

THE DEVELOPMENT OF ECONOMIC LIFE

As economic life has developed from that early stage in which men satisfied their wants by direct effort, that is, by producing for themselves what they needed to consume, to the highly complicated system of to-day in which everyone satisfies his own wants by satisfying first the wants of others, and in which people in every part of the world are contributing towards the supply of the various goods which will find a sale in the markets of countries far distant from their own, there has been the gradual opening out of an ever-widening gap between buyer and seller, between producer and consumer, the bridging over of which has necessitated the erection of an enormous economic structure, which has already been many centuries in building and which cannot by any means be said to be yet finished or complete. This structure consists of many parts, each one introduced to meet some special need which has arisen in connection with the economic development of society and each with a definite relation to the structure as a whole. The different parts of the structure, however, have for the most part been the work of persons acting independently of one another and actuated chiefly if not entirely by economic self-interest, and hence in spite of the attempts made at different times by States and Governments to remedy the defects of such haphazard building and, by exercising a control over economic forces and directing them into other channels, to make the structure conform to some more regular plan, it is not surprising that there should from time to time have existed a serious want of proportion between the different parts and that a process of self-adjustment should have been constantly taking place.

The following practical example will serve to illustrate the kind of gap which, in the majority of business transactions, exists between the original producer and the ultimate consumer. If someone were to order a pair of boots from a bootmaker living in the same town as himself, there would be actual personal contact between the producer and the consumer, but if, as may very well happen at the present day, a man living in a distant part of Canada likes to have boots of English make, and orders them through a local tradesman, the maker and the wearer do not in any way come into contact with one another and most probably do not even know each other's names. The knowledge that certain people in Canada are likely to buy English boots leads a Canadian importer to place an order for such boots with a merchant firm in London, which obtains the boots—shall we say—from a boot factory in Northampton. There is an enormous gap between the maker and the wearer and this gap is bridged by a structure of which the essential parts are merchants in both countries, transport agents, railroad and steamship companies, bankers, and perhaps many others. All of these perform their several parts without any idea that what they are doing is to help a particular Canadian settler to get just the kind of boots he prefers.

But all this elaborate arrangement was not set up in a day, or even in a century, and therefore, in order to get some clear idea of the way in which economic life has developed from the simple form of early days to the very complicated form of the present time, it is necessary to trace the steps by which all this has been accomplished.

I. In quite an early stage of economic life, such as that which went on in Anglo-Saxon times, local self-sufficiency was regarded as an ideal. The members of a village community formed a society in which there were to be found all, or almost all, the elements required for satisfying the simple needs of the people of that day. To a very large extent each household was able to provide its own food and much of what it required in the way of clothing, utensils, or furniture, but certain types of work had most probably come to be regarded as the occupation of specialists like the blacksmith, the wheelwright, the miller and the thatcher, who devoted their time to supplying services that were in general demand, and who received in return a portion of the food, etc. produced by others. In the towns this specialization was naturally much more highly developed than in the villages, for the very essence of the early town life was the greater economic interdependence that existed between the various members of the community.

The difficulty of securing a balance between demand and supply, as well as between the apparently conflicting interests of producer and consumer, led to the establishment of some kind of authority whose office it was to regulate the industry and the trade carried on within the walls or the boundaries of the town. In the more important towns this authority took the form of a Merchant Guild, a body of great power and importance, able not only to regulate the economic activities of the citizens but also to represent the town in its external relations with manorial lords or even with the King himself.

Craft Guilds, too, were formed, membership of which was confined to those who were working at the particular "mistery" or craft. They served as a protection to both producers and consumers, for whereas the interests of the latter were secured by very stringent regulations as to apprenticeship, materials used, and craftsmanship, those of the former were equally secured by reserving to the members of the guild the right of working at the craft and of selling the articles produced.

II. By degrees the members of the community became conscious of wants other than those which their own skill and resources could supply, and an exchange of commodities sprang up between the town dwellers on the one hand and those who lived in the country round, or who carried on their industry in other towns, on the other. This interchange of commodities involved a market, and in that market the conditions of buying and selling were regulated by the Merchant or Craft Guild or by some other established form of authority. This interchange of products between persons living in different places not only led to a further development of specialization and to technical improvements in the various crafts, for which one town or another might in the course of time have become famous, but it gave rise also to a new class of economic society, whose business it was to act as intermediaries between producers in the one place and consumers in the other, a class of persons in fact who bought to sell again. Amongst the earliest of these to emerge were the Drapers, or cloth merchants, the Grocers—so called because they dealt "en gros", or wholesale—who were buyers and sellers of all kinds of imported spices and drugs, and the Mercers and Haberdashers, who were retailers of various wares on a small scale.

Self-sufficiency still remained the ideal of the urban community, but it had become recognized that self-sufficiency could only be realized to a very partial extent, and that the members of the community might gain both in wealth and in convenience by their town becoming a market for the agricultural produce of the surrounding villages and for the wares produced in other districts and even abroad, which were brought to them and exchanged for the products of their own industry.

III. The area of commercial intercourse, which had been widened, as we have seen, by this bringing in of outside traders, extended little by little until a new ideal ousted that of local self-sufficiency and national self-sufficiency may be said to have taken its place. The King and his Council began to take an interest in trade, for trade could be made a means of bringing wealth into the country and of helping to fill the royal exchequer. Special trading privileges were granted to particular communities and laws were passed not only for the regulation of industry but also for the protection of traders, such protection being also extended to foreign merchants who brought to our markets the products of other countries, or who bought in our markets what their people at home would be ready to buy of them, whether in the way of our raw wool or of the products of our various crafts. In his foreign relations, too, the King had begun to discover the value of increased trade, and economic matters very soon began to enter into disputes with other countries, such as that which was partly responsible for the Hundred Years War with France. Thus the market was extended and the gap between producer and consumer grew wider and wider and already by the end of the fourteenth century it was becoming more difficult, though not as yet impossible, to adjust supply to demand and to ensure that what was produced would find a ready and profitable sale.

The great feature of mediaeval industry was its stability, and this is in very sharp contrast to the conditions which later on prevailed in the eighteenth and nineteenth centuries, when trade had begun to be subject to periods of alternate excitement and depression, and when a shortage of some things and a superabundance of others became a matter of common everyday experience.

IV. The transition from local self-sufficiency to national self-sufficiency did not take place without considerable social and economic upheaval. When the manorial system of village life with its clearly defined relations and duties began to break up, when the tenure of land in exchange for personal service was no longer general, new classes of people came into existence, viz. the tenant farmer who held his farm on payment of a rent, whether in money or in kind, and the free labourer who, no longer tied to the soil, could wander about the country in search of work, swelling as often as not the numbers of what were called the "valiant beggars", the fruitful source of recruits for the armies in France, or for the ranks of those ever ready to join in open rebellion, sometimes on political, sometimes on economic grounds.

This transition meant, too, the weakening of the old guild organizations in the town and the decline of their power and importance. When the royal regulations overrode those of the guild and the work had to be done in conformity with the wishes of a royal officer, such as the Aulnager, whose business it was to see that the woollen cloth was of the right width and texture, the guilds tended to become for the most part mere ornamental bodies, playing, no doubt, a part of some importance in the social life of the town but no longer controlling its industry and its trade.

The difficulties of this period of transition from local to national self-sufficiency were largely increased by the fact that a change in other directions was also taking place at the same time which had very serious effects on the conditions of rural life. This was the so-called "enclosure" movement. The scarcity of labour had already in the fourteenth century led to a certain amount of arable land being turned into pasture, but this movement of enclosure was considerably accelerated in the fifteenth and sixteenth centuries, when landowners began to find it much more profitable to grow wool than to grow wheat, with the result that some of the villages were almost depopulated and there was a very great deal of poverty and distress.

V. With the development of foreign trade under the Tudors, and its still more rapid rate of increase in the seventeenth and eighteenth centuries, we get a further widening of the economic gap, coupled, as was only natural, with considerable improvement in the machinery for bridging it. The voyages of adventurous navigators, and the attempts at colonization which followed the discoveries they made, led to an enormous expansion of commercial enterprise, rivalling that which Spain and Portugal had embarked upon nearly a century earlier and going on side by side with similar activity on the part of the French and the Dutch. The distant Colonies founded in the seventeenth century provided growing markets for the manufactures of the Mother Country as well as new sources of supply of shipbuilding requirements and of raw materials generally. The Navigation Acts of 1651 and 1660 tied these new markets to the Mother Country and thus prevented their being exploited by the merchants of other powers. These Acts provided that the trade between the Colonies and the Mother Country should be the monopoly of British shipping, and hence our mercantile marine was encouraged and the means of transport improved, while parallel with all this there was a development of the machinery of commerce, substituting easier modes of payment for the older method of goods for goods or goods for gold.

VI. This brings us to the eighteenth century, the period in which changes of a very far-reaching character began to take place. By this time economic life had become much more complicated, and the various forms of economic activity with which we are so familiar at the present day had begun to be much more clearly differentiated from one another, while those engaged in them were already tending to become separate sections of the economic community.

To begin with, manufacturing industry became definitely separated from agriculture. Under the domestic system weaving had been a second source of income to the farmer and spinning to the agricultural labourer. When the factory system was introduced, the products of hand labour could not compete with those turned out by the new machines working with the aid of steam power, with the result that these home industries gradually died out altogether. Farming, too, was undergoing a change of an almost revolutionary character. New and more scientific methods were being introduced which involved the use of larger capitals and which gave the death-blow to the old open-field system.

Banking, which in the seventeenth century had been a part of the business of the Goldsmiths, began in the eighteenth to develop as a highly specialized calling, the foundation of the Bank of England in 1694 having been followed by the establishment of private banks all over the country.

The business of insurance, formerly carried on by merchants and others, who found this a profitable way of employing their spare capital, also became specialized and "underwriting" emerged as a separate calling. The establishment of Lloyd's towards the end of the seventeenth century was followed in 1720 by that of the London Assurance Corporation and the Royal Exchange Assurance Corporation, and in this way was founded a form of business organization which plays such an important part in the economic life of the present day.

Already, then, by the end of the eighteenth century it may be said that specialization had reached an advanced stage, and when we bear in mind the development which had also taken place in coal-mining, in iron-mining, in the making of machinery, in shipbuilding, in the making of roads and canals, it is easy to understand how after 1815, when the twenty-two years of war with France were at last over, industry and trade were in a position to go ahead at a far greater pace than ever before.

The nineteenth and twentieth centuries have seen even more remarkable changes, the most striking of which perhaps have been in the matter of means of communication. The steamship, the railway, cheap postage, the telegraph, the telephone, electric power, motor transport, wireless telegraphy, the aeroplane, have followed one another in quick succession, and have tended in point of time to shorten the gap between producer and consumer, but at the same time, through the greater complexity they have brought with them, they have rendered the economic structure required to bridge it still larger and more elaborate than ever before.

There is another aspect of economic development generally to which attention may well be drawn. All the different forms of economic activity go on side by side and in close co-operation with one another, but they do not by any means develop at the same rate or in exact proportion to what business conditions require. Take, for example, the two complementary activities of Industry and Commerce, for in the relation which exists between them this unevenness of development is very conspicuously seen.

At one time the openings for commerce are greater than the power to produce the goods for which there is a demand, at another the arts of production seem to have gone ahead either of the means of transport or of the opportunities for disposing of the goods being turned out in such increased quantities. No sooner, however, do such discrepancies appear than economic forces set to work to adjust matters and to increase the supply of the service that happens to be lacking or falling behind. Here we have exemplified the tendency of economic life in general: it always seems to be perpetually struggling towards a condition of equilibrium which is, however, so elusive that, like the will-o'-the-wisp, it always appears to be immediately in front and yet to be continually receding.

The reason for all this is not difficult to find. The economic structure is not like a building with a single designer or a single architect. Those engaged in industrial, commercial or financial life direct their energies in whatever direction and at whatever time there seems to be a favourable opportunity for applying them profitably, hence progress in one direction is almost certain to outrun development in another. The conditions prevailing in the middle of the eighteenth century provide us with a very good example of this. The Colonies formed a large and ever-growing market for home products, but the power of production at home was limited by the amount that the worker could put out with his somewhat crude tools and implements and with the restricted amount of raw material at his disposal. But the demand, as it usually does, stimulated increased supply, invention resulted in the construction of mechanical appliances of a much more elaborate and advanced type, our huge coal deposits were utilized for the working of metals and the iron-fields of the Midlands became as a consequence a great source of national wealth. The natural forces of water and steam were called in to assist and supplement human strength and human effort; new sources of raw material were discovered and used.

All this meant such an enormous increase in the powers of production and such greatly enlarged output that the methods of transport proved inadequate for the trade which had now become possible. As a consequence canals were dug, roads were made, steam was applied to navigation and commercial intercourse became more rapid as well as more extensive. The extension of trade, again, led to developments in the financial system and reforms were introduced in currency and in banking. But there was always a tendency for some one of these developments to go beyond the point of immediate requirements, and hence there was a constant stimulus to that form of activity which for the moment had been left lagging behind.

The development of economic life can never be at a standstill. As the economic structure of society gradually changes, as the political and social ideals of one age give place to those of another, there has to be a process of constant readjustment. There must, in short, be the application of new means to new ends if the object of all economic effort is to be realized, namely, the ever-increasing satisfaction of human wants.

CHAPTER IV

THE FUNCTION OF CAPITAL

The part played by capital in the business world of to-day is so important, that it is well worth examining the term closely and impartially and in this way endeavouring to separate it from the prejudice which has unfortunately surrounded it owing to its use in political controversy.

THE TERM CAPITAL

The term capital has come to be used in at least four distinct senses, which may be briefly set out as follows:

(1) *The Economic.* Capital as a factor in the production of wealth.

(2) *The Financial.* Capital as money available for loans.

(3) *The Commercial.* The Capital of a Joint Stock Company.

(4) *The Political.* Capital as a section of the community whose interests are generally regarded as being opposed to those of Labour.

The first three of these are in common use in connection with business life. The fourth can hardly be regarded as a business term at all, but all the same it plays an important part in the relations which exist between employers and employed, and hence from the point of view of business life cannot be altogether excluded.

(1) *The Economic*

While economists at all times have been in general agreement in viewing capital as a factor in the production of wealth, they have varied greatly in their appreciation of the importance of capital and of its precise function in economic life. This is no doubt due in large measure to the influence of the economic conditions prevailing at the period in which each lived and wrote, resulting in emphasis being laid upon some particular aspect of capital.

With Adam Smith, for example, we get special attention drawn to the need for accumulated wealth. This follows upon his contention that improvements in productive capacity are dependent upon the extent to which Division of Labour is applied. He says:

> When the Division of Labour has once been thoroughly introduced, the produce of a man's own labour can supply but a very small part of his occasional wants. The far greater part of them are supplied by the produce of other men's labour, which he purchases with the produce, or, what is the same thing, with the price of the produce, of his own. But this purchase cannot be made till such time as the produce of his own labour has not only been completed, but sold. A stock of goods of different kinds, therefore, must be stored up somewhere, sufficient to maintain him, and to supply him with the materials and tools of his work, till such time at least as both these events can be brought about.[1]

This setting aside of a portion of a man's possessions for the twofold purpose of maintaining him, or those whom he employs, during the time required for production, and of providing the materials and tools necessary for production, is a conscious act. He decides not to devote all he has for the immediate satisfaction of his wants, but to use a part productively, and thereby secure for himself an increased income in the future.

But when he possesses stock sufficient to maintain him for months or years, he naturally endeavours to derive a revenue from the greater part of it, reserving only so much for his immediate consumption as may maintain him till this revenue begins to come in. His whole stock, therefore, is distinguished into two parts. That part which he expects is to afford him this revenue is called his capital. The other is that which supplies his immediate consumption.[2]

He thus brings out quite clearly the two fundamental ideas:

(1) That capital is wealth devoted to productive effort.

(2) That there is a direct relation between capital and income.

[1] Adam Smith, *Wealth of Nations*, Book II, Introduction.
[2] *Ibid.* Book II, Chap. I.

Adam Smith wrote at the very beginning of that period of industrial development generally known as the Industrial Revolution. John Stuart Mill, on the other hand, published his *Principles of Political Economy* when the factory system may be considered to have become definitely established. By this time capital had acquired a prominence in industrial life far greater than in the time of Adam Smith. Machinery and power-plant as well as the new forms of transport led to an ever-increasing demand for capital. Like Adam Smith, Mill lays stress on the industrial aspect of capital. "There is", he says, "another requisite without which no productive operations are possible, namely, a stock previously accumulated of the products of former labour."[1] Thus he associates capital with:

(a) Past industrial effort.

(b) Accumulation.

(c) Saving, for it is through saving that accumulation takes place.

It is to the necessity for bringing about an increase of capital that Mill draws special attention, connecting as he does any possible improvement in the standard of living of the working classes with an increase in that capital fund which he describes as being "devoted to the purchase of labour". "Wages", he says, "depend on the proportion between the number of the labouring population and the capital or other funds devoted to the purchase of labour; we will say for shortness the capital. If wages are higher at one time or place than at another, if the subsistence and comfort of the class of hired labourers are more ample, it is for no other reason than because capital bears a greater proportion to population."[2] This doctrine is generally known as the "Wage Fund Theory", and it can easily be understood that its advocates

[1] John Stuart Mill, *Principles of Political Economy*, Book I, Chap. IV.
[2] *Ibid.* Book II, Chap. XI.

laid very great stress on the importance of capital and more particularly on the increase of capital through saving.

Economic theory has undergone many changes since Mill's day and the "Wage Fund Theory" is no longer held. It is now generally recognized that wages are the workers' share of the product of the particular form of industrial activity in which they have taken part. Wages, like any other payment made in advance of the actual receipt of the price paid for the commodities produced, are provided out of capital, but the amount of capital which could be devoted to industrial undertakings does not determine the normal or average rate of wages.

Modern economic writers would agree with Mill that additions to capital arise through the deliberate postponement of the enjoyment of wealth. The service rendered to productive effort by this act of postponement is by some called "saving", by others "waiting". The motive for postponement may be prudence, or ambition, or merely the desire for a larger income and a higher standard of living in the future. But whatever the motive may be, we may associate the creation of capital with those attributes which Professor Marshall describes as productiveness and prospectiveness, and which may be said to govern the use of capital in ordinary business life.[1]

(2) *The Financial*

In the financial sense capital is more particularly associated with money loans which bring to the lender remuneration in the form of interest. This is capital in the sense in which it is used in the money market. Money may be borrowed for short or long periods. It may be used to assist production, or to make possible consumption in advance of income. From the point of view of the lender it is a means of obtaining income through allowing to others a temporary use of this portion of his wealth. From the point of view of the borrower it is getting the lender to render him a service, for which,

[1] Marshall, *Principles of Economics*, Book II, Chap. IV.

owing to the advantage he expects to derive from it, he is willing to pay.

This use of the term "capital" may rather tend to lend colour to the erroneous idea that capital and money are very much the same thing. Capital is, it is true, measured in terms of money, and money is used as a means of transferring capital from one person to another, but that is a very different thing from saying that these two things are synonymous. A business man will need to have a part of his capital in the form of money, and the financier will keep the whole of the capital which he is prepared to lend in this form. Both look to their capital to bring them in an income, and the particular form it takes is dependent upon the character of the business carried on.

(3) *The Commercial*

Every Joint Stock Company is formed with what is called an "Authorised Capital", the amount of which is stated in the "Memorandum of Association", though the whole of the share capital so authorized need not be issued, and, on the other hand, it may be increased by a resolution of the share-holders at an Extraordinary General Meeting. Capital in this sense simply means the amount subscribed by the share-holders, and it has nothing to do with the market value of the shares on the Stock Exchange at any particular time. It is, therefore, the sum of a number of contributions of capital by individuals who are saving this portion of their wealth and putting it into some particular business enterprise in the expectation of deriving an income from their investment. The capital thus subscribed will then be used by the company to carry on its business, and the fact that it is used for business purposes brings it under our first heading of capital in the economic sense.

(4) *The Political*

Much is said of the opposition of interest that is supposed to exist between Labour and Capital. The word capital as used in this phrase has a very different meaning from the three already described. Its use here is based on the assumption that in industrial life there are two organized and opposing forces known respectively as Labour and Capital. Labour we may take to mean the whole employed or wage-earning class, and Capital the whole body of those who control and direct industry in general, together with those who through ownership or control of capital are able to decide what work shall be done, how it shall be done, and how many shall be employed to do it.

The want of harmonious co-operation between these two groups is a very disturbing factor in industrial life. At all times it tends to diminish the productivity of the industrial undertaking. Both labour and capital, using the terms in the economic sense, are necessary factors in productive effort. The services of both must find their reward in the product derived from their joint effort. That product depends on the efficiency of the factors themselves, and on the way these factors are directed and controlled by the organizers of the business. The conflict referred to above is not that between the two factors or requisites of productive effort, but between the organized forces of the employees on the one hand, and the organized forces of the employers on the other.

From many points of view it would appear that the interests of Capital and Labour are not really opposed to one another. It is in the interest of both parties that business should be both active and profitable, and this result depends to a large extent on the harmony and goodwill with which the two forces co-operate. Industrial unrest, strikes and lockouts are a source of injury and loss to both. Much capital is immobilized and even wasted; much suffering and hardship are caused by loss of family income, and the industry itself may receive an injury from the effects of which it may take a very long time to recover.

CAPITALISM

The terms Capitalism and Capitalistic Production may be said to have come into use at the time of the so-called Industrial Revolution of the eighteenth century, which brought with it an immense increase of wealth on the one hand and an immense increase of poverty on the other. As already pointed out, one of the main industrial features of the changes then introduced was the increased use of capital, and it is not surprising therefore that to capital was attributed a great deal of the suffering and of the social disabilities which the new conditions brought to the working classes. Capitalism or Capitalistic Production was the term used by different writers to describe the new economic system and Capitalist was the name given to all the members of the class to the agency of which the evils were attributed.

What then is Capitalism? and what is a Capitalist? Many writers, opponents as well as advocates, of the different schools of socialistic thought, have tried their hands at giving some sort of definition, but there is the greatest difference of opinion as to what these terms really cover, and hence it may not be unprofitable, instead of examining the various views put forward from time to time on this subject, to try to elucidate what may be regarded as the essential attributes of these two terms.

To begin with it is fairly evident, from the fact that the chief aim of the very large number of people who support the Labour Party is often stated to be the substitution of Socialism for Capitalism, that these two systems are regarded as being mutually exclusive, not to say mutually opposed to one another. From this point of view Capitalism may be regarded as the general term applied to the present-day economic system, while Socialism, though this term is used to cover very widely differing schemes of political and economic reorganization, may be regarded as that applied to the alternative system which some by evolution, others by revolution,

would like to see put in its place. Further, since the avowed
aim of responsible socialists is to introduce the ownership by
the State of the instruments of wealth production, that is of
land and capital, together with State direction and control
of industry and commerce, finance and transport, Capitalism
as the opposite of this would seem to imply a system of individual ownership and individual control, and this is in fact
its main distinctive feature.

Apart from this outstanding difference as regards ownership and control it may be asserted that many features of the
present economic system are not peculiar to Capitalism, but
would appear also under a socialistic régime, for example, the
system of large industrial groups in which the workers do not
own either the material used in their work or the appliances
which assist them in it. Under either system the particular
task assigned to each worker is not determined by himself but
by some form of managing body, and the share of the product
which each would receive is to a large extent dependent on
circumstances over which he has no control. In short, the
existence of a permanently employed class, or the wage
system, cannot be regarded as a feature peculiar to Capitalism, though it may have become general as capitalistic industry developed. Thus the only really great difference
between the two systems in this respect would appear to be
that in the one case those employed are working under some
form of individualistic control with the profits, if any,
accruing to those who have supplied the necessary capital,
and in the other under an authority set up by the State and
under State control, industry and trade being carried on for
what those in authority conceive to be the interests of the
community as a whole.

THE TERM CAPITALIST

The term Capitalist may also be regarded as a product of
the Industrial Revolution, though the type of person it pre-

tended to describe had a much earlier existence. Even Adam
Smith, in his very careful analysis of capital and its employment, does not make use of the term. His typical employer
is the man who uses his own capital in his own business, and
profits, as the reward of capital, are apparently the income of
an employer of this type. For example, he speaks of "the
stock of the rich merchant" and again of "the people in
thriving towns who have great stocks to employ and who have
difficulty in finding the number of workmen they want". He
divides his employers into four groups, farmers, manufacturers, merchants and retailers, and that he conceives these
to be employing their own capital is evidenced by his remark:
"The persons whose capitals are employed in any of these
four ways are themselves productive labourers".[1] He treats
as a separate thing "the stock which is lent at interest",
distinguishing between what is lent for use as capital, that is
in industry or trade, and that which is lent out for consumption, that is to "the man who borrows in order to spend".
"As such capitals", he says, "are commonly lent out and
paid back in money, they constitute what is called the monied
interest. It is distinct, not only from the landed, but from the
trading and manufacturing interests, as, in these last, the
owners themselves employ their own capitals."[2] But after
the Industrial Revolution, the twofold character of the employer begins clearly to emerge. The early socialist writers
in particular distinguished between the employer as "Master"
and the employer as "Capitalist". One of these writers,
Thomas Hodgskin, in his *Labour Defended against the
Claims of Capital*, published in 1825, puts it in the following
way:

Masters, it is evident, are labourers as well as their journeymen.
In this character their interest is precisely the same as that of their
men. But they are also either capitalists or the agents of the

[1] Adam Smith, *Wealth of Nations*, Book II, Chap. IV.
[2] *Ibid.* Book II, Chap. V.

capitalist, and in this respect their interest is decidedly opposed to the interest of their workmen.

To Karl Marx, the capitalist is not merely the employer in another guise, but he is the exploiter of labour, who contributes nothing to the production of wealth, and yet takes a portion of it for himself. His theory is embodied in the well-known sentence: "All wealth is the result of labour, therefore, to the labourers all things are due". If we take "labour" to mean "human activity" and "labourers" a particular section of the community, the conclusion is by no means a logical one.

So long as the employer is using his own capital in his own business the necessity of giving him any distinctive name which should point him out more particularly as an owner of capital does not seem to arise. The income he derives from his productive effort is regarded as a whole and is not divided up in any way, but when it is definitely recognized that his function is a double one, that he renders service to the production of wealth both as the owner of capital and as the employer of labour, we find the nineteenth-century economists paying particular attention to the problem of distribution of income. Wealth they considered to be the product of three factors, land, labour, and capital, acting in combination with one another, land covering the gifts of nature, labour the human element, and capital the stored-up wealth, the result of previous economic effort. To those who contribute these factors are given the respective names of landowners, capitalists, and productive labourers. "Each of these classes as such", says John Stuart Mill, "obtains a share of the produce: no other person or class obtains anything except by concession from them. These three classes are considered in political economy as making up the whole community."[1] Since Mill's day, however, the development of the Joint Stock Company, and its taking the place to a large extent of the private concern as

[1] John Stuart Mill, *Principles of Political Economy*, Book II, Chap. III.

the type of business enterprise, has necessitated a more complete separation between the functions of management and capital. The manager has tended to become a salaried official rendering a highly specialized form of labour service and the term capitalist is reserved for those who provide capital for the undertaking, who in the last resort exercise control and who receive profits as their share in distribution.

From what has been said it should be evident that the term capitalist involves something more than the mere possession of capital, it involves as well the placing of it at the disposal of others. In the Middle Ages, under the domestic system of industry, the weaver, for example, owned his own loom and probably also the wool which he was turning into cloth. These were forms of capital, but their possession did not make him a capitalist. It was the Industrial Revolution that brought the capitalist into industry, the man who had the means and the enterprise to start, shall we say, a weaving mill in which many weavers worked under his direction, using his looms and his raw material. The capitalist emerges when ownership of the means of production, that is of capital, passes from the individual worker to those who provide the buildings, the machinery, the plant, the raw material, for the use of all members of the new industrial unit.

The conflict of interest which then developed between Capital and Labour seems to have divided economic society into two classes, employers and employed. Before the changes of the eighteenth century there was not for the most part any clear line of social distinction between masters and men. The master craftsman was the final or complete stage of industrial life, and it was the ambition of every apprentice sooner or later to be a master himself. The introduction of the factory system, however, with its large groups of workers employed in the same building, and working in connection with machinery driven by steam power, completely altered this state of things, and the tendency from this time onwards has been the erection of a barrier between the two industrial classes, transition from the one to the other being the exception rather than the rule. The main factor in bringing about this change was undoubtedly the large amount of capital the new methods necessitated. The employer must either own a considerable amount of capital himself or be able to induce others to entrust their capital to him. The employed had not this advantage. Thus the employing class tended to become more or less closely associated with the idea of Capital and the employed class with that of Labour, and this led to the former being frequently spoken of as Capitalists.

THE FUNCTION OF THE CAPITALIST

Having followed in this way the evolution of the capitalist, we are now in a position to consider a little more closely the part he plays in the world of business. To begin with, it may be said that the capitalist emerges in response to a demand for a particular type of service, in other words, he supplies a recognized want. The introduction of machinery and of steam power made it necessary that work should no longer be carried on by individuals, but by groups. The factory system, as has been already pointed out, involved the use of large capitals, larger of course than the individual worker could supply, larger even as time went on than the employer himself could provide. Besides, it must not be lost sight of that capital is required for the business as a whole, for the use of an industrial group, and no part of it can be considered as allotted to any individual worker.

It is clear then that the new type of business required someone to organize the effort, and someone to provide the capital. But since the new type of industry was more speculative than the old, that is to say, the difficulty of adjusting supply to demand was much greater, someone was required to take the risks and this duty devolved naturally upon the capitalist.

Under these altered circumstances the individual worker ceased to be an independent tradesman, and he became part of an organized group, working under direction and control. He performed his own allotted task and was not concerned with finding a market or with gauging its requirements.

The function of the capitalist having under modern conditions become a necessity, the question is, who is to play the part? The answer goes to the root of the controversy between socialists and individualists. There would seem to be four alternatives. The function of the capitalist may be performed by

(1) The employer himself, the actual owner of the business.

(2) The employees associated together in a given undertaking, each owning some part of the capital.

(3) A body of shareholders, as in a Joint Stock Company.

(4) The State.

The first of these is not uncommon, especially in the smaller type of business. The second has been tried from time to time, but the experiments in so-called productive co-operation have met with very little success. The third is at the present day the usual type in all larger concerns, and to a certain extent also in smaller ones. The last forms part of the socialist programme, which includes State ownership of the means of production, distribution and exchange. With the tendency of the business unit to get larger and larger, it would seem that the choice will lie between the two last named, that is between private ownership of capital, by the members of the community, and public ownership of capital by the State. In either case the source of capital would be the same, namely a portion of wealth produced and set aside for fresh production, but in the former case saving is voluntary, in the latter it would have to be compulsory.

ECONOMIC PROGRESS

The introduction of what has been called the Age of Capital brought in its train a considerable social upheaval, but the use of the term Industrial Revolution for the changes involved in the transition from a domestic system to a factory system must not be taken as indicating that the movement was a sudden or violent one. The changes were in fact gradual and partial. Many writers regard the period of transition as having lasted from 1770, when Hargreaves invented the spinning jenny, to 1840, when the use of machines and steam power had become fairly general. But during this period of seventy years the movement, at first very slow, gradually advanced more and more rapidly as one industry after another was industrialized. Of the gradual nature of the industrial development the business of cotton spinning provides a very good example. Taking the figures of the import of raw cotton as an indication of the growth of the industry we find that

For the years 1771–75 the average was 4¾ million lbs.
,,　　1776–80　　　　,,　　　6¾　　　,,
,,　　1781–85　　　　,,　　　11　　　　,,
,,　　1786–90　　　　,,　　　25½　　　,,
For the year 1800　the import was 56　　　,,
,,　　1810　　　　　　,,　　136½　　　,,
,,　　1840　　　　　　,,　　406　　　　,,

while in 1920, some eighty years later, it was about 1900 million pounds or nearly five times as much. At the same time the industrial unit has in general become larger and larger, machinery has become much more highly specialized, and the effect of progressive mechanical improvement has been that tasks involving heavy physical effort as well as those requiring great technical skill are now being performed by machines. All this means the extended use of capital, and as the object of introducing the machines is to reduce costs, and to get a given amount of output with less expenditure of human effort, the whole tendency of so-called labour-saving machinery and appliances, whether in the workshop or in the office, is to reduce the amount of labour employed on any particular piece of work and so, at any rate temporarily, to cause unemployment. This result, however, is not necessarily a lasting one, for the cheapening of the production may lead to much greater demand, and many instances could be given in which a larger and not a smaller number of workers have been employed after the introduction of a new machine than were employed formerly. If one were to look at the question from the point of view of the community as a whole without reference to the individuals which compose it, one would be inclined to argue as follows: the extended use of capital in industry, especially when it takes the form of new types of machinery, increases the total amount produced and hence the average amount per person employed. Or it may be put in another way, namely, that, owing to the total real income of the community having been increased, the average real income per person is also increased and thus this extended use of capital has brought with it an improvement in the standard of living generally. On the other hand, it is quite possible that in certain cases the productive advantage derived from the use of new inventions may be more than wiped out by additional costs incurred in connection with their adoption. The current number of an American business paper, *Bradstreet's Weekly, A Business Digest*, which has come to hand while this page is being written, contains an article headed "Use of Machinery Lowers Labour Costs in Shoe Industry", which is so much to the point that with the editor's permission it is being quoted here almost *in extenso*.

Use of Machinery Lowers Labour Costs
in Shoe Industry

Progress has always been at the expense of suffering. The evolution of man to a highly civilized state has only been accomplished through the cruel process of natural selection—the survival of the fittest.

To the shoe factory worker out of a job, and there are now 25% of the number employed during 1923–25 in such a state, the thought of progress must be remote. The 75% still at work, with earnings cut a third by lower wages and part-time work, can have little appreciation of it.

Shoes are obviously a necessity. The production of boots and shoes has been very little reduced during the depression, though it has become much more spasmodic. Total output in 1931 was only $12\frac{1}{2}$% below 1929, and only 4% below the 1923–25 average. Thus far in 1932, the rate has been only 2% less than in 1931.

This is a decided contrast to the behaviour of pay-rolls. During the first seven months of this year these averaged little better than half of what they were in 1923–25.

The average rate of wages has been going slowly down hill since the beginning of 1927. The wage rate, however, has not been the only factor. The labour cost per unit of production (which is the result of dividing pay-rolls by production) has since 1928 been declining more rapidly than the wage rate. Wage rates are one important element of this unit labour cost. The other is the output per hour of the worker.

Beginning in 1928, this efficiency began to rise, but it was not until 1931 that an important change took place. In that year, however, output per man per hour increased over 11% above 1930. Slight progress has been made this year.

Measured, therefore, by unit labour costs, the industry has become highly efficient. As far as labour cost is concerned, the expense of making a pair of shoes is now down to almost half what it was seven years ago. This, of course, has been the result of increasing use of machinery and of improvement in the use of that machinery. Machinery, moreover, would seem to be the main cause of the falling wage rate. That is, it has made possible the replacement of skilled, high-wage labour by unskilled, low-cost workers.

Whether this substitution of machinery for men in this industry has been economically sound is a question which cannot be answered here. Capital and overhead costs obviously have been

increased. Whether they have been increased more or less than
the saving in labour costs could only be determined by exhaustive
research. The rather small reduction in the wholesale price of
shoes during a period of sharply lower hide and leather prices,
however, would suggest that not much had been gained.

At all events, progress in labour efficiency has been gained,
probably never to be lost. If the labour no longer needed in producing our shoe necessities could now be rapidly shifted to other
occupations, a definite contribution to our standard of living would
be made. These workers, moreover, must somehow make a change,
since, unlike the majority of the unemployed, they cannot look
forward to much increase in production with a recovery from the
depression.

Unfortunately, probably a large proportion of these men are
highly skilled craftsmen, who, because of this specialization, know
no other trade. This is quite generally true of most of the victims
of technological unemployment. It is one of the penalties of our
method of progress through specialization.

THE COST OF PROGRESS

The above-quoted article provides an admirable illustration
of the general principle that no economic change takes place
without cost to someone. It is of the very essence of any improved productive process that by its introduction labour can
be saved. If labour is saved, someone is displaced, at any
rate temporarily, and displacement causes loss and hardship.

Yet without change there can be no progress. The term
progress as applied to economic life needs a certain amount
of explanation. We may put it in this way: since economic
effort aims at obtaining the satisfaction of wants, that effort,
from the economic point of view, may be regarded as most
successful which brings the greatest amount of satisfaction,
and economic progress may be taken to mean an increase in
the amount of satisfaction obtained from a given expenditure
of effort. The object of every economic change is to secure
some gain, but this gain is seldom secured without some
accompanying loss and so, looked at in this way, progress
would mean a net gain on balance.

It does not do, however, to take a purely material view of progress. Looked at in this way the gain would be estimated as so much additional output from the employment of a given amount of labour and capital. But the loss may be something less material and less calculable, for in addition to loss of wages to those who lose their employment and loss of capital due to old machinery becoming valueless, both of which are calculable, there is the suffering and hardship caused to those thrown out of work and the physical and moral effects of the possible lowering, even though it may only be temporary, of the standard of living, and both of these are incalculable.

Leaving aside, however, this aspect of economic change, and looking only for the moment at the material advantages to be obtained by a business undertaking through its making use of new inventions and improvements in processes, it should be borne in mind that every such improvement does not necessarily result in a net gain to those who have introduced it. We may assume for the sake of argument that no new labour-saving device would be installed in the factory or office if it were not expected to be more economical in its working, that is, that it would be likely to result in lower production costs and through the saving thus effected would enable the business to compete on better terms in the home and foreign markets.

Competition acts as a stimulus to improvement in method, for no one can afford to be left behind in the great struggle of business life. If a manufacturer did not continually improve his mechanical equipment he would find it increasingly difficult to obtain orders at a remunerative price and in the end he might even find it necessary to close down his business altogether. The gain of any improved process may be regarded as being the difference between the capital charges due to the new machine and the advantages to be derived from using it; but against this will have to be set the loss which there would be if there were some unused value in the machine it displaces. This idea of an unused value will be made clearer by a practical example. Let us suppose that when the old machine was introduced the advantage at the time of such introduction was calculated on the assumption that it would last ten years and in the company's accounts depreciation was allowed for year by year on this basis. If this machine were in its turn to be replaced at the end of the ten years there would be no unused value, but if the replacement should occur at the end of say five years there would be an unused value in the old machine which would have to be set against the advantage expected to be derived from the use of the new one which was taking its place.

What has happened of late in a good many businesses is that improvements have followed one another in somewhat rapid succession, so rapid in fact that the cost of one new machine has not been covered before another is introduced in its place. The greater the depression in trade the greater the effort to reduce costs by new labour-saving devices, and, by cutting prices, to secure as large a share as possible of the shrunken market. New businesses will be equipped from the start with the latest improvements, old businesses must follow suit or they will be unable to compete.

The result is twofold: on the one hand the capital loss arising out of this rapid succession of improvements tends to cripple the undertaking financially, and on the other there is no time between the successive displacements of labour caused by the various improvements for that labour to be reabsorbed as a consequence of that trade expansion which is generally expected to follow the cheapening of the product. Hence both capital and labour have suffered and the diminished profits of the one and the increased unemployment of the other have served to intensify the general economic depression.

PART II

BUSINESS LIFE AND INSTITUTIONS

CHAPTER V

THE JOINT STOCK COMPANY

From the foregoing short survey of the economic side of life, that is of business life in its more general aspects, we must now pass to a consideration of the actual conditions under which business in its more technical sense is carried on.

Two outstanding features at once claim our attention:

1. The ever-increasing size of the business unit, with its large capital and its highly developed organization.

2. The complexity of business relations, which requires the head of any large industrial or commercial undertaking to be a man of outstanding capacity, with, in addition to his grasp of the details of his own particular business, a knowledge of finance and of world trade movements.

A century ago a company with a capital of £10,000 would have been considered quite a large undertaking, at the present day a capital of £1,000,000 would not be considered anything out of the ordinary.

Complexity has followed almost naturally upon this increase in the size of the business unit, for the wider field of operations brings with it special problems of its own. With the larger scale on which business is conducted comes greater specialization of functions, and the consequent demand for greater skill in co-ordinating the many forms of effort which have to be brought into combination with one another.

There is complexity also in the structure of business. Take, for example, an important manufacturing concern, working with a large capital and sufficiently established to be able to increase that capital when suitable opportunities for employing it present themselves. Such a company will not infrequently endeavour to acquire the ownership or control of adequate sources of raw material. It may also establish works or selling organizations in foreign countries, forming subsidiary companies for the purpose. In various other ways, too, it is apparent that, compared with even a few generations ago, the typical business unit is now larger and more complicated than it was, and its management and direction demand a greater amount of knowledge, skill and resource.

As a necessary accompaniment of this development we have the growth of the Joint Stock Company and the establishment of the principle of Limited Liability. The large business requires outside capital; the public are invited to take shares in the concern; those who subscribe the capital required demand, not unreasonably, to know the extent of their liability, and since 1862, when an Act was passed to facilitate the issue of shares with limited liability, this system has become almost the general rule.

Many enterprises, it is true, are still carried on by a single person or by two or more persons in partnership, but for the most part these are on a comparatively small scale. Such businesses are as a rule managed by a proprietor or proprietors, who either own the capital employed in the undertaking or borrow it at an agreed rate of interest. All profits which may be made belong to them, and on them also falls the burden of loss should such be incurred.

The modern business, however, whether mining or manufacturing, whether commercial, financial or transport, is frequently on too large a scale for private ownership. Too large a capital is required and the uncertainties of business are too great. In a limited liability company the capital is subscribed by a number of shareholders, who in a greater or less degree, according to the type of shares they hold, and the extent of their holdings, take upon themselves the risks of the enterprise. But for individuals to combine for the purpose of using their capital to the best advantage is not by any means a thing of recent origin. In the Middle Ages the risks of domestic trade were known and limited and the conditions of production and selling were regulated in every detail by the Merchant or Craft Guild. But with the development of foreign trade new situations arose. English merchants in foreign cities were often exposed to harsh treatment, possibly also to the seizure of their goods and even to imprisonment as well. As far back as the reign of Edward III, for example, the English merchants carrying on the wool trade in Flanders found that, in order to protect effectively their individual interests, some form of association was almost a necessity. Many companies of merchants of this type appear to have been formed in the fourteenth century. They were probably not very different in character from the guilds with which they had been associated in their home town or city, for membership carried with it certain trading rights and privileges, and some assurance of protective action should such become necessary. These companies assumed the form of somewhat close corporations of subscribing members each trading individually with his own capital and in his own interest. The fifteenth century, too, provides many examples of merchant companies formed for mutual pro-tection of their members. In the foreign markets where English merchants were carrying on their trade, these companies of Merchant Adventurers, as they were called, had each a recognized area or country to which its operations were confined and in which its members enjoyed special trading privileges. A great impetus was given to this movement by the discoveries of Columbus, the Cabots and Vasco da Gama, and by the many other explorers who in the sixteenth century were encouraged to emulate the achievements of those named. Many of those who took part in, or helped to fit out, the various expeditions were merchants who had definitely in view the expansion of their trade, and hence, as soon as openings were made for commercial enterprise in any part of the world, it was not long before a company of Merchant Adventurers was formed to protect the mutual interests of those merchants who were ready to take advantage of the openings thus provided. In this way during the sixteenth and seventeenth centuries regular trading connections were established and trading companies formed in many parts of Asia, Africa and America. The way merchants and explorers combined in enterprises of this type may be illustrated by one or two historical examples. In *Hakluyt's Voyages*, for instance, we read of the expedition of Hawkins to Brazil in 1530 which resulted in the trade opening it provided being utilized by a company of Southampton merchants. Again, a few years later, in the days of Edward VI, there was the famous voyage of Chancellor and Willoughby, who aimed at discovering a North-East passage to the Indies and at developing an East Indian trade by that route. The enterprise was due to a company of London merchants formed to carry out the scheme. Together they subscribed a capital of £6000 in shares of £25 each. As is well known, the Adventurers failed to reach their objective; they did not, as a matter of fact, get beyond Archangel, where they established an important trading centre. This Russian Company, as it is called, may be regarded as the genesis of the Joint Stock Company, for in it we have an association of merchants contributing their capital to a common stock in order to carry out an enterprise too vast and too dangerous for any of them to carry out individually.

By the end of the sixteenth century two essentially different types of company could be clearly distinguished, viz. the Joint Stock Company and the Regulated Company. In the former, merchants put their capital into a common stock and traded as a single body; in the latter, the merchants who were admitted as members of the company paid an annual subscription, but retained their individuality as trading concerns. Belonging to a company conferred on its members the privilege of trading in the particular area covered by the company's charter. The Regulated Companies were exclusive bodies and this was much resented by outside merchants who frequently attempted to trespass on the companies' preserves. In the seventeenth century there was much conflict between these independent merchants, interlopers as they were called, and the members of the companies, and it not infrequently happened that they were able to get royal support for their claim to break through some company's monopoly. The Merchant Adventurers is one of the best examples of a Regulated Company. But there were many others, such as the Eastland Company, trading with the Baltic, and the Levant Company, trading with the Eastern Mediterranean.

The most distinguished of the Joint Stock Companies was the East India Company, a powerful corporation established by a charter granted in 1600 by Queen Elizabeth for the purpose of trading with India and the far East. At first it took the form of a Regulated Company, but twelve years later the merchants who were members of it decided to put their capitals into a common fund and thus made of it a joint stock enterprise. The seventeenth century saw a very great development in our foreign trade; but the greater the number of merchants engaged in trading in distant markets, the more difficult it was for the Regulated Companies to preserve their monopoly, and they consequently fell gradually into disuse. The Joint Stock Companies, on the other hand, had a more permanent existence, the East India Company, for example, not being disbanded till 1858, after the Indian Mutiny. Starting with the establishment of trading stations or "factories" in India and beyond, this company came later to acquire a territory in Bombay that formed part of the dowry of Katherine of Braganza, the queen of Charles II. Quarrels with the native states led to the company having to maintain an armed force in India, and it was not long before it was involved in a contest for supremacy with the French East India Company, which had developed on similar lines. In a succession of wars, one state after another was annexed, until the carrying on of the combined functions of sovereign and trader, as Adam Smith describes them, often with mutually conflicting interests, proved a task far beyond the capacity of the company, and, as before mentioned, the Indian Mutiny led to its dissolution.

The extension of the joint stock principle to industry was a consequence of the Industrial Revolution. The introduction of machinery and steam power, the increase in size of the business unit, and the larger capital required in the new factories, led to outside people being invited to take a share-holding interest. Already, before the middle of the eighteenth century, the idea of admitting the general public, even those having no interest in or knowledge of the particular business with which the undertaking was concerned, had become fairly generally recognized in companies formed for the purpose of trade and industry. Buying and selling of shares on the London Stock Exchange became very general and stockbroking developed into an organized profession with its own headquarters and settled rules as to membership and management. The orgy of speculation which, towards the end of 1720, resulted in the crash known as the South Sea Bubble, indicates how popular gambling on the share market had become even at that date.

Somewhere in between the purely trading company and the purely industrial company is the type of company in which the merchants of a town formed an association and contributed their capital for the purpose of securing benefits common to all those taking part in some particular industry. For example, there is the case of the Norwich weavers, who in 1555, finding that the finer types of cloth made in Italy were taking the place of their native worsteds, subscribed the necessary capital for bringing in Italians who would teach the Norwich craftsmen their art, with the result that, before long, these cloths were made cheaper and better in Norwich than the imported Italian makes, to the benefit of the whole industrial community of that city. This is a very early example of the formation of a joint stock company for the promotion and encouragement of industrial enterprise.

In 1711 the South Sea Company was formed with the object of trading in the "South Seas". The fantastic estimates of enormous profits led to the wildest possible speculation in the company's shares, and at one time the £100 shares changed hands at as high a price as £1000. This encouraged the flotation of a large number of other companies, many of which were merely fraudulent attempts to extract money from a too credulous public. The character of such bogus concerns is well illustrated by the following examples: one had as its object the importation of "a Number of Large Jack Asses from Spain"; another was formed "For the transmuting of quicksilver into a malleable and fine Metal"; while a third, the most outrageous of all, perhaps, was "For an Undertaking which shall in due time be revealed". Subscribers to this last scheme who deposited £2 a share were promised £200 a year for each share they took up. It is hardly necessary to say that the whole affair was a hoax, and that the promiser, after having received subscriptions from quite a large number of persons, promptly disappeared with the money.

The crash came in the autumn of 1720, but Parliament, alarmed at the recklessness with which the gambling in shares was being carried on, and at the frauds that were being committed by many of the promoters, had already taken action in the matter with a view to exercising a control over the formation of new joint stock companies and the objects for which they were started. In the spring of 1720 the so-called "Bubble Act" was passed, requiring that all companies wishing to raise capital through the issue of transferable shares should first obtain a charter of incorporation from the Crown or, alternatively, a special Act of Parliament. These incorporated companies were based on a principle which, at the present day, has become almost universal, namely, that the liability of the shareholders should be limited to the amount of capital they subscribed. In the second half of the eighteenth century an attack was made on the Mercantile System, and on the policy of regulation and restriction associated with it. This attack was as much for philosophical as for practical reasons, the doctrine of natural liberty or *Laissez-faire* having found many adherents in England, largely as a result of the teaching of Adam Smith. On the one hand, there were those preaching that Government regulation of industry was contrary to the law of nature, and on the other hand, there were those pointing out that the wide extension of trade and the new methods in industry were incompatible with the restrictions which might have found some justification at an earlier date. Amongst the many laws restricting trade which were repealed in the early years of the nineteenth century was the Bubble Act already referred to. As a consequence of its repeal in 1825 it became a much easier matter to obtain the necessary charter of incorporation for a joint stock company, but, at the same time, under the new Act, the limited liability principle was abandoned. The reason advanced for this step was that it was unfair to the general public for the liability of the shareholders to be limited, for, under that system, when a company became bankrupt, all that the creditors could get out of the liquidation were the realizable assets. Consequently the Crown, in granting charters of incorporation, was given the power of attaching a condition that the members of the company, that is the general body of shareholders, were collectively and individually responsible for all the company's debts. This was a considerable check to the development of the joint stock company movement, for who would dare to become a shareholder in a company with the knowledge that if the company failed he or she might become liable for the whole of that company's losses?

The next step forward was in 1844, in which year an Act was passed enabling companies to be formed by a much simpler procedure. Instead of the old cumbersome and expensive method of applying to the Crown or to Parliament for a charter, all that was necessary was to obtain a Certificate of Incorporation.

A still further advance was made when in 1855 the policy laid down by the Act of 1825 was completely reversed and once again the principle of limited liability was introduced by Act of Parliament, but the clause in the Act which forbade the issue of shares of a nominal value of less than £10 very much restricted the class of persons to whom an investment in these companies was open and limited also the area to which the joint stock principle was applied. In 1862, however, the £10 limit was removed, and it is from that year, therefore, that we can date the beginning of the general establishment of joint stock companies with limited liability as the accepted type of industrial and commercial organization. The removal of the £10 limit gave a tremendous impetus to saving and investment, for it enabled quite small sums to be used in subscription for shares, the owner having the knowledge that once the instalments were paid, no further demand could possibly be made upon him.

From what has been said so far about legislation introduced for the regulation of joint stock companies it would appear that at one time the main object was to protect the shareholder, and at another to make it easier for business enterprises to acquire the necessary capital. For example, the Bubble Act of 1720 aimed at making it more difficult for bogus companies to be floated of the type that was causing such scandal at that time. The necessity of obtaining incorporation, which then became law, secured at any rate some scrutiny of the objects for the pursuance of which the public were being asked to subscribe. The provision made in the same Act for limiting liability afforded further protection to the shareholding public.

On the other hand, when repealing the Bubble Act in 1825, there was clearly the intention to make the flotation of new joint stock companies less difficult and so to assist the development of those larger industrial units the introduction of which was one of the outstanding features of the Industrial Revolution. There was, however, some discouragement to investment in such companies through the power that was given to the Crown of rendering the shareholders in the company personally liable for its debts.

Again, the Act of 1844 was evidently designed to facilitate the formation of new companies, while in that of 1855, with the return to the principle of limited liability, protection of the interests of the shareholders seems to have come more prominently forward. The Act of 1862 merely carried this a step farther by making it possible to get capital from a larger public.

More recent legislation has tended in the main to introduce greater definiteness into:

(1) The mode of forming an incorporated company.

(2) The object for which the company is formed.

(3) The registration of companies and the supervision by the Board of Trade which registration involves.

(4) The form and contents of the prospectus of the company.

(5) The conditions under which the shares may be issued.

(6) The rights of the holders of the different classes of shares.

The most recent of the Companies Acts is that of 1929, consolidating the various Acts relating to joint stock companies passed between 1908 and 1928 in addition to introducing several amendments, more particularly in the matter of the responsibility of directors to the shareholders whose capital they are appointed to administer.

In the Act of 1929 there are very strict regulations as to

(1) The keeping of a register of members.

(2) The holding and conduct of meetings.

(3) The keeping and auditing of accounts.

(4) The appointment of directors, their duties and their liability for their actions.

(5) Informing the shareholders of the true financial position of the company.

(6) Winding up the company in the event of liquidation.

The first thing is to get a clear idea as to how a joint stock company is formed and operated and then, when this is done, we shall be in a better position to take up some of the various matters covered by the headings just given.

THE FORMATION OF THE COMPANY

Though the Companies Act provides for the formation of companies in which the liability of the shareholders is unlimited, it is sufficient for our purpose to consider only companies in which the liability of the shareholders is limited by the amount of capital individually subscribed, that is to say, companies the titles of which are obliged by law to contain the word "Limited".

Limited Liability Companies may be of two kinds, public and private; a public company is required to have a minimum of seven members, this being the legal term by which the shareholders are designated. A private company may not have more than fifty members and not fewer than two. A private company, moreover, may not issue any invitation to the public to subscribe for its shares. It is readily understood, therefore, that in a great many cases companies are public, though, with some few exceptions, the provisions of the

Companies Act apply equally to public and private companies alike.

Those wishing to form a company must append their names to what is called a "Memorandum of Association", at least seven signatures being required for a public company and two signatures for a private company. This "Memorandum of Association" must state the name of the company, where its office is situated, and for what objects the company has been formed; it must further set out the amount of the capital, the class of shares it is proposed to issue, and the nominal value of each.

With the "Memorandum" it is necessary to register what are called the "Articles of Association". These are in effect the detailed regulations for the management of the company. The "Articles" may either be in the form attached to the Companies Act and known as "Table A", or they may be a special set of articles embodying some or all of the articles in "Table A", but at the same time making provision for the special circumstances or requirements of the particular company.

If it is desired at any time to alter one or more of the articles this must be done by "Special Resolution", that is to say, by a resolution passed with a three-quarters majority at an Extraordinary General Meeting called for this purpose.

The "Memorandum" and "Articles of Association" must be deposited for registration with the Registrar of Companies, who will issue a Certificate of Incorporation. When this has been received the company is considered to be duly formed and is free to carry on business in accordance with the requirements of the Companies Act.

When appealing to the public to provide the necessary capital for the new undertaking a prospectus is drawn up, and after it has been handed to the Registrar for registration it forms the invitation to people generally to apply for shares in the company. The prospectus is required to give very full information about the new company, with names and addresses of directors and auditors, and all such information as is necessary to acquaint would-be subscribers with the nature of the business and what it is proposed to dó with the capital when subscribed. By issuing the prospectus, the directors and other persons responsible for such issue render themselves liable under the Act for any untrue statement made in it, and thus the public are protected against any fraudulent attempt to obtain capital from them on false pretences.

Applications for shares having been received, the next step is for the company to proceed to allotment. This takes the form of a letter addressed to each of the shareholders informing him or her of the number of shares allotted. It is usual for a certain portion of the money to be paid on application, a further amount on allotment, and the balance at intervals as stated in the prospectus. For example, in the case of a company issuing £1 shares, it would not be unusual for 5s. to be paid on application, a further 5s. on allotment, and the remainder in equal instalments at intervals of one or two months, as the case may be. It sometimes happens that the company does not call up all the outstanding instalments as it may not be in immediate need of the amount of capital which these would provide, but when such calls as are made have been met, the company issues share certificates bearing the seal of the company and the signatures of one or more directors of the company, together with that of the secretary, to the effect that the particular shareholder is the registered proprietor of a specified number of shares.

Shares are not all of the same description. The two main classes are known respectively as ordinary and preference, though these may themselves be subdivided, as for example some ordinary shares may be described as "Deferred Ordinary", and some preference shares as "Cumulative Preference". Special conditions of issue are attached to each class of share, the difference between them consisting more particularly in the matter of their claim to receive a dividend, should the profits obtained permit of such being paid, and their claim to a share of the assets in case of liquidation. Differences also sometimes exist in the matter of the voting rights which members in virtue of the shares they hold can exercise at the general meetings of the company.

THE REGISTER OF MEMBERS

Every company is obliged by law to keep a register of its members, that is, of the shareholders, showing the number of shares held by each, when those shares were acquired, and, if they were parted with, at what date the transfer took place. In addition, every public company must keep an index of this register so that the shareholdings of any member at any particular time can be readily ascertained. The register and index must be kept at the registered offices of the company and must be open to inspection. An annual return containing a list of past and present members must be supplied to the Registrar of Companies after the close of each financial year, together with a certain number of other particulars concerning the share capital.

THE HOLDING AND CONDUCT OF MEETINGS

The General Meetings of the company afford the members an opportunity of coming together and hearing something of the company's affairs. The first of these meetings is the Statutory Meeting, which must be held within three months from the date at which the company is entitled to commence business.[1] At least seven days before that meeting the directors must issue to every member what is called "The Statutory Report", giving the shareholders information as to the total number of shares allotted and the extent to which they have been paid for. In this report the Board is also required,

---

[1] Companies Act, 1929, Section 113.

amongst other things, to make a statement of the financial position of the company as it exists at that time.

The Annual General Meeting is the great opportunity for the shareholders to express their views as to the general condition of the company's affairs and to pass any comments or criticisms on the way those affairs have been managed. An Annual General Meeting must be held, as its name implies, in every calendar year and in any case it must not be more than fifteen months after the preceding General Meeting. Notices of the Annual Meeting must be sent to all the shareholders at least seven days before the date fixed for the meeting, and with it the directors must issue a report and balance sheet for the past financial year. The notice sets out in brief form the purposes for which the meeting is called; these generally include the following:

(1) To receive and consider the directors' report together with the balance sheet and profit and loss account which are attached to it.

(2) To declare a dividend (if any).

(3) To elect directors.

(4) To elect the auditors and fix their remuneration.

(5) To transact any other ordinary business of the company.

At the meeting the agenda consists of the items set out in the convening notice. The Chairman presides and he is supported by the other members of the Board. The proceedings are opened by the Chairman calling upon the secretary to read the notice convening the meeting and the auditors' report which is appended to the balance sheet. Then follows the most important item on the agenda—the Chairman's speech, in which he explains in detail the various items in the balance sheet and profit and loss account, gives some account of the past year's trading operations and as a rule ventures some forecast as to what may be expected in the coming year.

He then moves the adoption of the report and accounts and this is seconded by one of the other directors. After this the meeting is open to discussion, and when this is ended the resolution is duly put to the meeting and except in such cases as there is a majority opposed to it, and this is very unusual, is declared by the Chairman to have been carried.

The election of directors covers

   (1) The election of new directors.

   (2) The re-election of retiring directors.

   (3) The confirmation of the election of directors appointed since the last Annual Meeting.

As a rule the auditors offer themselves for re-election, and as they are in a special sense the guardians of the shareholders' interests, the resolution is proposed and seconded by members who happen to be present at the meeting.

THE KEEPING AND AUDITING OF ACCOUNTS

The auditors' report, to which reference has already been made, is a very important document. It is an assurance to the shareholders that the financial position as disclosed by the directors is correct in every particular. Under the Companies Act the auditors in their report are obliged to state

   (1) Whether or not they have obtained all the information and explanation they require.

   (2) Whether in their opinion the balance sheet is properly drawn up so as to exhibit a true and correct view of the state of the company's affairs according to the best of their information, and the explanations given to them, and as shown in the books of the company.[1]

Before the auditors can give such a report as this, it is evident that they must have had access to the company's books of account and to all the minutes, correspondence and

[1] Companies Act, 1929, Section 134.

documents which throw light on the various transactions which have given rise to the entries in those books.

The auditors are as a rule properly qualified and registered accountants, for the work they have to do is of a highly technical character and involves not merely checking the accuracy of the book-keeping of the company's officials, but also a critical examination of its financial methods with a view to satisfying themselves that the accounts do as a matter of fact show exactly what the company's position really is. It has been already pointed out that the auditors are responsible to the shareholders and not to the directors and that it is to the former that they must render an account for their actions, but at the same time they may be and generally are of great assistance to the directors, for their advice and guidance are often sought when questions of detail arise in connection with the carrying out of the Board's financial policy.

EXTRAORDINARY GENERAL MEETINGS

In between the Annual Meetings, Extraordinary General Meetings may be convened by the directors of the company when there is some special business to put before the members, such as the increase of the company's capital or the alteration of its articles. It is also permissible for the shareholders themselves, if a sufficient number of them make the requisition, to demand that the directors shall convene such a meeting. This latter course would hardly be taken unless the shareholders felt that they had some particular reason to be dissatisfied with the way the directors were conducting the company's affairs. The resolutions passed at such meetings are "Special Resolutions", the terms of which must be stated in the notices convening the meetings, and which cannot be passed unless three-quarters of the members voting are in favour of them.

THE MINUTES

It is obligatory upon every company to keep a record of the proceedings at all general meetings, whether annual or extra-ordinary, as well as of those at the periodical meetings of the Board of Directors or of the management. These records are known as the "Minutes" and the book in which they are entered is the "Minute Book".

The Minutes when entered have to be confirmed by the directors and signed on their behalf by the Chairman or by the director who in his absence happens to be presiding. It is usual for a draft of the Minutes to be circulated amongst the directors after any meeting for their approval or criticism, and then in their final form they are produced at the next Board Meeting for confirmation and signature. Confirming and signing the Minutes of the preceding meeting is as a rule the first business on the agenda paper at any meeting of the directors.

The Minutes when confirmed and signed may be regarded as evidence

(a) That the meeting was held on the particular date,

(b) That the resolutions put to the meeting were duly carried, and

(c) That other transactions or discussions which took place were as recorded.

THE DIRECTORS

A word should now be said about the relative position of shareholders and directors. The directors, as their name implies, direct the conduct of the company's affairs. They decide upon the policy to be followed and they exercise a general supervision over the administration, but it is the shareholders, the providers of the capital, who have the ultimate control. This power they exercise at General Meetings, when they may refuse to adopt the report and accounts, to re-elect directors or auditors, or to pass the special resolutions submitted to them. They may even demand the dismissal of individual directors or of the Board as a whole and may call for the appointment of a committee to examine into the company's policy, position and past transactions.

Apart from such investigations, which are only called for when serious trouble is feared, the shareholders' knowledge of the company's business is gained from the reports issued to them from time to time by the Board of Directors. In them, therefore, it is essential that they should be able to place implicit trust. They themselves are the company, so to speak, but as they appoint the directors with full power to manage its affairs for them, they have to a large extent to leave the fortunes of the company in their hands. Hence, before investing money in a given undertaking, shareholders would do well, in addition to ascertaining the past results, the present position and future prospects of the company, to satisfy themselves that those who are at the head of the concern, that is to say the directors, are people in every respect worthy of their confidence, and that in their hands the interests of the company may safely be left.

The original directors whose names appear on the company's prospectus have accepted office at the invitation of the promoters of the enterprise, but their remaining in office depends on their being able to retain the confidence of the shareholders, for when at the Annual Meeting their names are put forward for re-election, those present can refuse to renew their term of office.

A director may be invited to join a Board for various reasons, for instance, it may be that he has a special knowledge of the industry or business concerned, and of its special requirements, in other words, he may be an expert. Or again, he may be chosen for his general business experience which would enable him to take a broad as well as a practical view of the subjects which might come before the Board for discussion.

The Board of Directors may be described as the Executive Council of the company; with it, as already pointed out, lies the decision on all questions of policy; it lays down what has to be done and how. Its resolutions cover such matters as the financial arrangements which have to be made with the company's bankers, the entering into of contracts or legal agreements, alterations in manufacturing methods, contemplated extension of buildings or plant, and reorganization of work or of staff. Many routine duties also are forced upon the directors by the Companies Act, including responsibility for the keeping of Minutes, the keeping of registers, the making of returns and the calling of general meetings.

The Board not infrequently finds it desirable to delegate to certain of its members the direction or supervision of some particular branch of the work. For this purpose small committees are formed for dealing with financial, technical, legal or other matters; such committees are often empowered to take decisions when waiting for the next meeting of the Board, but such interim decisions need to be confirmed by the Board at its next meeting. The carrying out of the policy laid down by the Board of Directors, the administrative as contrasted with the executive function, is the task of the management. The successful and smooth working of the enterprise depends very largely on the good understanding and spirit of loyal co-operation between these two bodies.

THE MANAGEMENT

Immediately responsible to the Board and working in close contact with it is the Managing Director, who being both director and manager is the link between the company and those it employs. The Managing Director—in some companies more than one may occupy this position—keeps the Board informed at its periodical meetings of what is taking place and how the business is progressing. In this way close touch is maintained between those who plan and those who execute, between those who decide what shall be done and those who issue the necessary instructions and see that those instructions are duly and efficiently carried out.

Functioning immediately under the Managing Director are the General Manager and the various Departmental Managers, such as the Sales Manager, the Works Manager, etc., according to the particular type of business. Each is responsible for his own particular department, but the co-ordination of their several branches of activity rests with the Managing Director.

THE SHAREHOLDERS

As a rule the directors are themselves holders of shares, and it is usual for the Articles of Association to specify a minimum number of shares which a director must hold, these being known as "Qualification Shares". He may hold more than this number, but he is not obliged to do so.

In many companies, if not in most, the great majority of the shares in the company are held by the outside public, who occupy a position somewhat analogous to that of sleeping partners, inasmuch as they take no active part in the general direction or management. At the same time they can, and often do, exercise a very real and effective control over the company's affairs, for, as mentioned above, they can at General Meetings express their approval or disapproval of the policy that is being pursued by the Board, and by their votes they are in a position to accept or reject the resolutions submitted to them.

CHAPTER VI

THE KEEPING OF ACCOUNTS

In a very early stage of human society there arises the problem of the establishing of a balance between income and expenditure. Man very soon passes from the stage in which he satisfies his wants by direct effort into that in which he can only satisfy his own wants by first satisfying those of others. The substitution of a money economy for one of barter introduced a new element: one of time as well as of method. Each transaction is no longer regarded as something complete in itself, but as being one of a series of transactions which together bring in an income which can be expended in satisfying the daily wants as and when desired. A produces wheat and sells portions of it from time to time to B. With what he gets from B he is able to buy from C, D, E and F what is required to satisfy the needs of his household, and under such conditions it is evident that the sale of the wheat to B, which brings to A what we may call his income, is a necessary preliminary to the satisfaction of his wants, while the net result of the transactions sets a limit to the amount of satisfaction he can obtain.

Even if A's business were as simple as that described, some system of account-keeping, however primitive, would become almost a necessity. In the first place it is only the net gain from the sale of the wheat which forms A's income, and which consequently he is free to expend in satisfying his needs. To arrive at this net income involves a certain amount of calculation, and this will become the more evident if A sells wheat to many persons at different times and at different prices. Without a record of the transactions this calculation would be almost impossible. The net income which he derives from producing and selling wheat is the sum which remains over after capital has been replaced and all expenses of production have been allowed for.

On the expenditure side, also, it is equally necessary to keep some accounts, for purchases are made from time to time, and it is the sum total of such purchases over a period such as a year which has to be brought into relation with the income over the same period. Consequently, if A is to be in a position to know where he stands financially, to know whether or not what he sells is being sold at a profit, whether or not the total amount received from his sales of wheat is greater or less than what he spends on producing it and whether or not he is living beyond his means, he must keep accounts both of his business incomings and outgoings and of his own personal income and expenditure.

In early life, even before the period of earning an income is reached, it is not unusual to keep a strict account of how money received as pocket money or as personal allowance is expended; and the same applies to the housekeeper who receives a weekly sum for household expenses. Such account keeping is useful, for it provides a record not merely of how the money has been spent, but also of how it is distributed over the various classes of wants and thus supplies material for drawing up what is known as the family budget.

In times when education was less general, and comparatively few could read or write, accounts were kept in an extremely primitive way, such as by chalk marks on the wall or by notches on a stick. It can well be imagined that the mediaeval yeoman, craftsman, or innkeeper would have resorted to such simple methods as these for recording the debts of his customers and his money matters generally; but more important people, like the merchant or the manorial lord, would doubtless have had a clerk or official of some kind to keep a record of the incomings and outgoings of the business or estates, and of this the numerous manorial rolls which still exist afford ample evidence.

The best examples of mediaeval book-keeping, however, are to be found in the Pipe Rolls of the Exchequer, the national account-books of the day. The Court of the Exchequer was that department of the King's Council whose business it was to receive the royal revenues and to keep the record of national income and expenditure. All the transactions of this Court and the statements of account submitted to it were entered upon the rolls of parchment known as the Pipe Rolls of the Exchequer. An exceedingly detailed account of this Court and its proceedings, of its various officers and their duties, is to be found in a very remarkable document called "Dialogus De Scaccario" or "The Dialogue of the Exchequer".[1] This dialogue is between a supposed master and pupil, and it is through the answers of the master to the somewhat naïve questions of the pupil that we get so much valuable information about this institution.

As to what the Exchequer was and why it was so called, we may well turn to the Dialogus itself:

Pupil. What is the exchequer?

Master. The exchequer is a quadrangular surface about ten feet in length, five in breadth, placed before those who sit around it in the manner of a table, and all around it it has an edge about the height of one's four fingers, lest anything placed upon it should fall off. There is placed over the top of the exchequer, moreover, a cloth bought at the Easter term, not an ordinary one but a black one marked with stripes, the stripes being distant from each other the space of a foot or the breadth of a hand. In the spaces moreover are counters placed according to their values; about these we shall speak below. Although, moreover, such a surface is called exchequer, nevertheless this name is so changed about that the court from sitting at the exchequer is now itself called the exchequer; so that if at any time through a decree anything is established by common counsel, it is said to have been done at the exchequer of this or that year. As, moreover, one says to-day "at the exchequer", so one formerly said "at the tallies".

Pupil. What is the reason of this name?

Master. No truer one occurs to me at present than that it has a shape similar to that of a chess board.

---

[1] Compiled in the twelfth century by Richard Fitz-Nigel, Bishop of London, and Treasurer of the Exchequer. Given *in extenso* by Bishop Stubbs in his *Select Charters*.

The Court of the Exchequer met twice a year at Easter and at Michaelmas and on each of these occasions the Sheriffs —the "shire-reeves"—who were the King's representatives in the different counties or shires, had to appear and render an account of their stewardship. At the former meeting the Sheriff would present his accounts and pay into the Court an instalment of the annual revenue, receiving by way of receipt what was known as a "tally". The "tally" was a rectangular piece of wood about nine inches in length, in which notches were cut marking the pounds, shillings and pence received. This stick was then split down the middle, the two halves being exactly alike as to the width and number of the notches cut. The width of the notch denoted the particular sum which it was desired to record; thus a very wide notch indicated £1000, a less wide one £100, and so on down to a mere nick which represented a penny. One of the halves was given to the Sheriff by way of receipt, and the other half was kept by the Court of Exchequer, so that a check was established on any possible tampering with the "tally" on the part of the Sheriff who received it.[1] At Michaelmas, when the accounts of the year were finally made up, the Sheriff produced his "tally" as evidence of what he had already paid on account. At the same time he made a statement of all the payments he had had to make on the King's account, and these were allowed him against what was called the "ferm of the Shire", that is the composition sum agreed upon for all the revenues which the Sheriff had to collect. As already stated, the proceedings of the Court, including all the statements of account, were then entered in the Pipe Rolls, one of which was kept by the Treasurer of the Court, another by the Chancellor and a third by a legal officer representing the King.

From these Rolls it can be seen that the same basic prin-

[1] An illustration of a tally in use so late as 1819 is given in Dr W. Cunningham's *Growth of English Industry and Commerce: Early and Middle Ages*, p. 157.

ciple of account-keeping was in force then as is the case at the present day. What the Sheriff received, that is the amount agreed upon as being the "ferm of the Shire", was placed to his debit. What he paid out, either into the Treasury, or to the various persons to whom sums of money were due from the King, or what he had disbursed in settlement of tithes, alms, or other charges on the royal manors in his district, was placed to his credit. If the payments he had made did not amount to as much as what he had received, there remained a debit balance against the Sheriff which he had to make good, or else it was carried forward against him to the next year's accounts. If there was a balance the other way he could claim it from the Court. The following extract from the Pipe Roll of the County of Huntingdon is a very good example of account-keeping in mediaeval times.[1]

	£	s.	d.	£	s.	d.
Pagan the Sheriff renders account of £48. 10s. 7d. of the ferm of Huntingdon for last year	48	10	7			
	£48	10	7			
Paid in Treasury (blanched)				30	14	2
and in payment to Ralph Waspal (blanched)				17	16	5
				£48	10	7

The term "blanched" requires explanation. The amount paid in as the "ferm of the Shire" could be reckoned in one of two ways—either by "tale", i.e. by merely counting it, or by testing it, i.e. by melting it down, a process known as "blanching". In order to cover the risk of the coin paid in by tale being deficient in silver, it was usual for the Sheriff to collect an additional sum of one-twentieth, which was known as "blanching money".

---

[1] Cunningham, *Growth of English Industry and Commerce: Early and Middle Ages*, p. 160.

From this account of the book-keeping of an earlier age, we must pass to our main subject of book-keeping and the part it plays in the business life of the present day. The subject is a highly technical one, and it may be said with reason that to explain its intricacies should be left to a professional chartered accountant, but it is no part of the plan of the present work to provide a textbook on book-keeping, business management, or any of the subjects required by those embarking on a business career. This is merely an introduction to business life as a whole, and hence it is proposed to give only just such an outline as will enable the reader to grasp and to take an interest in the general features of business life and the relation of the various parts of it to one another.

The simplest form of account-keeping, and one which is more or less familiar to every individual, is that which provides a record of personal income and expenditure, but in this, as suggested above in connection with the Sheriff's accounts, will be noticed the same fundamental principle of placing on the debit or left-hand side everything that is received, and on the credit or right-hand side everything that is paid out. The underlying idea is that the individual whose income and expenditure are being accounted for is a debtor for what he receives in the sense, not that he is in debt to anyone for this amount, but that it is something for which he must account to himself, and hence, if it is possible to conceive such a thing, he is his own debtor to this extent. Similarly, for what he pays out he is treated as being his own creditor, inasmuch as he can claim from himself a recognition that he has made these payments on his own behalf. For the purpose of account-keeping, the person himself is treated as an outsider, and hence there will be found no difference in this respect between his own account of daily receipts and expenditure and that which appears in his pass-book at the Bank, in that the Bank is debited with what is paid in by the customer and credited with everything that is drawn out.

An account of this private or personal kind is in reality a sort of Cash Book, for it is a record only of cash received and cash paid out. It enables one to see at any time exactly how one stands as regards the cash position, that is, how much has been received, and how much has been paid out, and whether anything remains over. The advantage of keeping such an account is obvious. For example, the householder knows that on certain particular dates there will be claims to be met for, say, rent, rates and taxes, school fees, insurance premiums, etc., and from the state of the Cash Book it will be readily seen whether a sufficient balance for these outgoings is being kept in hand, and then on the basis of the income that is likely to be received, and the other items of expenditure that are likely to be incurred before these claims have to be met, it will be possible to calculate what provision for them has to be made in advance.

A Cash Book does not, however, provide all the information which the private accounts may be required to afford. For instance, it may be desired to ascertain how much during the year is spent on such various forms of expenditure as rent, food, clothing, fuel, education, etc. For this further accounts would have to be kept. The entries on the credit side of the Cash Book must be transferred to another set of accounts each with a heading appropriate to the particular subject, not omitting one for sundries, that is, for items which it is difficult to classify. These separate accounts when added up should of course show a total amount equal to the sum of the items on the expenditure side of the Cash Book. In this way, in addition to the information afforded by the separate accounts, a check is provided on the accuracy of the account-keeping in general.

With one's private affairs the keeping of accurate accounts may be regarded as a very desirable and useful habit, but in business life it is very much more than this, for no business undertaking can be carried on without a properly arranged accounting system, and in the case of a joint stock company, which is carried on with the capital subscribed by the outside public, it is a necessity imposed by law, and any failure to comply with the legal requirements renders those responsible liable to heavy penalties. The Companies Act of 1929 makes this clear in the following terms:[1]

(1) Every company shall cause to be kept proper books of account with respect to
   (a) all sums of money received and expended by the company and the matters in respect of which the receipt and expenditure takes place;
   (b) all sales and purchases of goods by the company;
   (c) the assets and liabilities of the company.

(2) The books of account shall be kept at the registered office of the company or at such other place as the directors think fit, and shall at all times be open to inspection by the directors.

(3) If any person being a director of a company fails to take all reasonable steps to secure compliance by the company with the requirements of this section, or has by his own wilful act been the cause of any default by the company thereunder, he shall, in respect of each offence, be liable on summary conviction to imprisonment for a term not exceeding six months or to a fine not exceeding two hundred pounds:
   Provided that a person shall not be sentenced to imprisonment for an offence under this section unless, in the opinion of the court dealing with the case, the offence was committed wilfully.

The main and ultimate object of account-keeping is to make it possible at any time to ascertain precisely the exact financial position of the firm or company: whether the business is being carried on at a profit or a loss; whether the business is advancing or declining; whether expenditure is properly controlled. The books of account, however, serve another and very useful purpose, for, if properly kept, they are a storehouse of information which can be constantly utilized by the management for the efficient carrying out of the daily work.

[1] Companies Act, 1929, Section 122.

For example, information can be obtained from this source to show the relative importance of the different branches of the business; the profitableness or otherwise of new processes; the amount of business done with particular customers and their regularity in the matter of payment. Accurate records of this kind are essential to a well-conducted business, and it is in the books of account that they are mostly to be found.

For such purposes it is evident that a mere record of receipts and payments, such as the Cash Book used for one's private income and expenditure, would be entirely inadequate. From a Cash Book we can at any moment see the cash position and how it has been arrived at, but it does not show what is owing to the company or what is owed by it, and does not show whether individual transactions are profitable or the reverse. An entry on the debit or left-hand side of the Cash Book may be to the effect that £500 has been received for goods sold, but the tradesman in question may be selling goods which he happens to have in stock and which at the time of sale he has not paid for. All the same, so far as the Cash Book is concerned, he would be able to show an increased balance in hand. This serves to illustrate the general statement that if in any business money has been received in payment for something with regard to which indebtedness has been incurred but not yet met (whether for goods bought or for services rendered), the fact that the cash position is improved is no criterion as to the prosperity or otherwise of the business.

Here again, although this involves a certain amount of reiteration, it is as well to emphasize the fact that money received from the sale of goods cannot be regarded as net income, for against this has to be set not only the cost of the goods themselves but also the remuneration for the services rendered by all those who in one capacity or another have taken part in the work of selling.

In the case of a merchant, for example, it is not unusual to say that his profit is the difference between buying price and selling price, but even this statement requires qualification, for to the buying price must be added all the various expenses incurred in connection with the carrying on of the business. In the case of a manufacturer, too, we could only arrive at the net profit after deducting from the selling price a sum for the replacement of capital which would be sufficient to cover the cost of raw material, and in addition a due proportion of the cost of replacing the fixed capital, such as buildings, plant, machinery, etc. Moreover—and this applies to any type of business—all wages and salaries paid have to be taken into account, and so also have such items as interest on loans, cost of transport, current office expenses, etc., etc.

Calculations such as these considerations involve can only be made with accuracy where there is a proper system of accounts. Without one it would not be possible to arrive at the net income of the business, or to ascertain whether in fact there has been any net income at all.

BOOK-KEEPING BY DOUBLE ENTRY

Business accounts are kept for the most part under the system known as book-keeping by double entry, the essential feature of which is that for every transaction there must be recorded in the books of the firm or company both a debit and a credit entry. To every transaction there must be two parties, and as every transaction may be looked at from the point of view of the one party or the other, it may be said that every transaction has a double effect on the business. But is it quite clear what, for the purpose of book-keeping, is regarded as constituting a transaction? A practical example will perhaps help to make this clear.

John Brown & Co., Wholesale Provision Merchants, London, have placed with Henry Smith & Co., Importers of Canned Fruits of Liverpool, an order for two hundred cases of tinned peaches each containing two dozen at 10s. a dozen. Terms—cash one month after delivery.

From a book-keeping point of view, paradoxical as it may seem, here are two transactions, not one.

(1) There is a transaction in goods:
Henry Smith & Co. parts with £200 worth of tinned peaches and John Brown & Co. receives them.

(2) There is a transaction in cash:
for a month later John Brown & Co. parts with £200 and Henry Smith & Co. receives that sum.

Since then

(a) to every transaction there must be two parties,

and (b) the account receiving something is debited and that paying out is credited,

it is not difficult to understand how it is that, as stated above, "for every transaction there is both a debit and a credit entry".

This being established, we can go a step further and say that the sum total of all the debit entries will exactly correspond with the sum total of all the credit entries, and, as a natural corollary, the balances of the individual accounts when extracted from the Ledger will comprise debit balances (i.e. excess of debits over credits) exactly totalling the credit balances (i.e. excess of credits over debits). This process of extracting the balances of all the individual accounts is known as "preparing a Trial Balance", and if the debit and credit totals are not in agreement, then it becomes evident either that some error has been made in the figures themselves, or that some entry has been made on the wrong side of an account. Thus, by a system of book-keeping by double entry, there is provided a very efficient control over the accuracy of the accounts.

BOOKS OF ACCOUNT

THE LEDGER

The principal account book is known as the "Ledger". In this book separate accounts are kept for each of the different persons or firms with which the company has business, whether as buyer or seller—these being known as "personal" accounts; as well as for wages and salaries, for cash, raw materials, capital expenditure, investments, goods purchased, etc., etc.—all these being known as "impersonal" accounts. Every transaction will be recorded in two of these accounts, one on the debit side and one on the credit side, the one on the debit side representing what has been received, and the one on the credit side showing what has been parted with.

THE CASH BOOK

The Cash Book, as has already been described, is a record of cash received and cash paid out. As the Ledger is the principal book of account, and as such contains a record of all transactions, the cash account would in the ordinary way be one of the accounts in the Ledger. But as the passing of money enters into almost every transaction, the number of receipts and payments would be so great that it is generally found convenient to keep a cash account in a separate book known as the Cash Book. It is, however, to all intents and purposes a Ledger "impersonal" account and is treated as such.

SINGLE ENTRY

In a small business it is sometimes found sufficient to keep the accounts by a system of single entry. Under these the Ledger is practically the only book kept and the accounts in it are limited to "personal" ones. There may be in addition a Cash Book as a record of cash transactions, but entries will be made direct into one or other of these books. Further, as the only accounts in the Ledger are for the persons or firms dealt with, there will only be a single entry for each transaction.

BOOKS OF PRIME ENTRY

Under a system of double entry, transactions are not entered direct into the Ledger as in the case with single entry but they are transferred to the Ledger from what is generally called a book of "prime entry",[1] such as the Journal or one of the substitutes for it mentioned below. In the Ledger there will always be inserted, in a column set aside for this purpose, a reference to the particular book from which the entry was transferred, so that if necessary it can be checked at any time. The usual procedure, therefore, is to record every transaction in the Journal or other book of prime entry and from it, to use a technical term, to "post the Ledger".

THE DAY BOOK

At this stage it would be well to consider what the sources of information are likely to be which form the basis of the various entries in the books of account.

All transactions of a firm, whether sales or purchases, and all receipts of payments of any kind will be recorded in one form or another, and these records, or copies of them, will always have to pass through the hands of those whose business it is to keep the accounts. As regards goods bought by the firm, the order will either be contained in a letter or be entered on a specially prepared order form. In either case copies will be kept in the company's files and from them the appropriate entries will be made. As regards the sale of goods, an invoice will always be sent to the customer at the time the goods ordered are dispatched, and copies of these also will be kept and dealt with in the same way.

When a Bill of Exchange is drawn or accepted, a record will be kept of the transaction. When wages or salaries are

[1] Sometimes spoken of as "books of original entry" or "subsidiary books".

paid, a receipt or voucher will be given for each such payment, and the same applies to all purchases for cash. When
payments are made by cheque, there is an entry on the counter-
foil. When tools or materials are taken out of the storeroom,
a receipt or voucher is given for them. In short, for every
transaction there is in the office a record of one kind or other,
and it is from these records that the entries are made in the
Journal or other book of prime entry.

It is sometimes found convenient to keep a kind of diary,
sometimes called a Day Book, in which transactions of any
sort or kind are entered in the order of their occurrence, and
when such is kept it is from this book that entries in the
Journal are made instead of from the various documents
concerned.

THE JOURNAL

The Journal has certain special features of its own, and
amongst other things it is important to notice that

(1) It is a book which contains those entries necessary to
record the internal transactions of a business, and for
every transaction there is a record of the accounts to be
debited, and those to be credited.

(2) Moreover, it is a book that can be used to record any
such transaction, since all transactions involve a debit
and a credit; but where the transactions are all of a
similar nature, such as goods bought or goods sold, it
is found of greater convenience to keep the record of
these latter transactions in special journals of their own.

These books are known as

A Bought Day Book[1] *or Purchase Journal*, in which all
purchases are entered—the supplier being credited, and
the stock or some other account being debited.

[1] The Bought Day Book and the Sold Day Book must not be confused with the Day Book referred to above, which is merely an
unclassified daily register of transactions.

A Sold Day Book[1] *or Sales Journal* in which all sales are entered and the customer debited, and the stock or some other impersonal account credited.

When, however, only one Journal is used, it is commonly known as the General or Transfer Journal. A special importance attaches to this book, inasmuch as it may contain entries of a more or less confidential nature.

As an example of this "General" type we may take the transactions connected with John Brown & Co.'s purchase of tinned peaches from Henry Smith & Co., which would be entered very much as follows:

JOURNAL OF JOHN BROWN & CO.

Date	Particulars	Folio	£	s.	d.	£	s.	d.
1932 March 1	Goods Dr. To H. Smith & Co. Being purchase of 200 cases of tinned peaches	10 25	200	0	0			
						200	0	0
April 1	H. Smith & Co. Dr. To cash	25 6	200	0	0			
						200	0	0

It is more usual, however, at the present day to use separate Journals for Sales and Purchases, and hence to illustrate what may be called the modern method of book-keeping, a list of imaginary transactions is appended with notes as to how they should be entered in Cash Book, Journal and Ledger.

It will be noticed that every transaction appears in the Journals as both a personal and an impersonal entry, the personal entries being posted individually to their appropriate accounts in the Ledger and the impersonal entries only in monthly totals.

[1] See note 1, p. 89.

RECORD OF TRANSACTIONS
first half of January 1932

1932		£	s.	d.
Jan. 1	Received payment by cheque of our account with John Simon for goods sold and invoiced to him, 24. xi. 31	154	11	6
	This amount would be entered on the debit side of the Bank Cash Book, then paid into the Bank. Afterwards it would be posted from the Cash Book to the credit side of John Simon's account, thus forming the double entry:—Bank: Dr.—J. Simon: Cr. (see the Cash Book).			
2	Cheque drawn on our Bank and forwarded to W. Noakes & Co., for goods received and invoiced by them, 3. xii. 31	57	8	9
	This amount would be entered on the credit side of the Bank Cash Book and then posted to the debit side of W. Noakes & Co.'s account, thus forming the double entry:—W. Noakes: Dr.—Bank: Cr. (see the Cash Book).			
4	Goods received from Watfield & Co. this day. (Entered in Purchase Journal.) Invoice No. 1	50	0	0
5	100 1-cwts. Soap sold to Duncan & Sons this day. (Entered in Sales Journal.) Invoice No. 1 ...	200	0	0
6	Machine supplied by Armstrong & Co. (Entered in Purchase Journal.) Invoice No. 2	100	0	0
8	Gas and Coke supplied by Gas, Light & Coke Co. (Entered in Purchase Journal.) Invoice No. 3	25	0	0
10	L.M. & S. Rly Co. account for Carriage. (Entered in Purchase Journal.) Invoice No. 4	10	0	0

12	50 1-cwts. Soap at 40s. per cwt. ...	100	0	0			
	50 pkts. Wax Candles at 1s. 6d. per pkt.	3	15	0			
		103	15	0			
	Carriage	1	0	0	104	15	0

Sold to Parkinson & Co. Ltd. Invoice No. 2

PURCHASE JOURNAL

1932	Sundry creditors	Inv. no.	Ledger folio	Personal Accounts £ s. d.	Goods £ s. d.	Plant £ s. d.	Gas £ s. d.	Carriage £ s. d.
Jan. 4	Watfield & Co.	1		50 0 0	50 0 0			
6	Armstrong & Co.	2		100 0 0		100 0 0		
8	Gas, Light & Coke Co.	3		25 0 0	5 0 0		20 0 0	
10	L.M.S. Rly Co.	4		10 0 0				10 0 0
				185 0 0	55 0 0	100 0 0	20 0 0	10 0 0

Ledger folio: *Posted to the individual A/cs. in Purchase Ledger. (Cr.)*

Posted to Impersonal Accounts in Total (Dr.)

[The Impersonal Account to be debited should be marked by someone in authority on the invoice.]

SALES JOURNAL

1932	Sundry debtors	Inv. no.	Ledger folio	Personal Accounts £ s. d.	Sales Accounts £ s. d.	Carriage £ s. d.
Jan. 5	Duncan & Sons	1		200 0 0	200 0 0	
12	Parkinson & Co. Ltd.	2		104 15 0	103 15 0	1 0 0
				304 15 0	303 15 0	1 0 0

Ledger folio: *Posted to individual A/c in Sales Ledger. (Dr.)*

Posted to Impersonal Accounts in Total (Cr.)

[The Impersonal Account to be credited should be marked by someone in authority on the invoice.]

CHAPTER VII

PRESENTING THE ACCOUNTS

The previous chapter was concerned with the subject of account-keeping in general and ended up with a practical example to illustrate something of book-keeping methods. We must now pass to what is the real purpose of all this amount of work and consider the uses to which the information contained in the accounts is usually put.

The first and most important use is undoubtedly to provide the material for the annual financial statements from which the partners or shareholders may learn the financial results of the year's trading. But there is a hardly less important use and that is to provide information regarding current business for the use of the Board of Directors and the Management. These purposes are for the most part served by three different forms of financial statement.

(1) *The Balance Sheet.*

This is usually the annual statement of accounts prepared after the close of the financial year and submitted to the shareholders at the Annual General Meeting. It aims at exhibiting to the shareholders what the company's financial position really is.

(2) *The Profit and Loss Account.*

This is also prepared annually and submitted to the shareholders with the balance sheet. Its purpose is to show whether the year's trading has resulted in a profit or a loss and what the balance is one side or the other.

(3) *The Trading Account.*

Trading accounts are confidential statements usually prepared monthly, or at other stated intervals, for the use of the Directors and the Management, their object being to set out clearly the results of trading during the period in question and how they have been arrived at. This form of statement is additionally useful when it includes a comparison between the results achieved in a particular month or period and the corresponding period of the previous year. Material for a further comparison is afforded when, in addition to the monthly results, those for the portion of the financial year which has elapsed are also added and compared with the same portion of the previous year.

It is convenient to take the last of these Accounts before dealing with the other two.

THE TRADING ACCOUNT

The object of this account is, as already said, to show periodically, not merely the gross trading profit, but in addition the net result of carrying on the business. If a Trading Account, therefore, is to be really useful it must fulfil both of these requirements, that is to say, it must be something more than a mere Trading Account, it must be a Profit and Loss Account as well. As, however, the latter term is generally reserved for the annual account of that nature prepared for the shareholders, it will avoid confusion if the form of combined statement we are now considering is simply styled "The Trading Account".

One of the clearest, and therefore best, forms of such an account is that which starts with the total amount received from sales during the period concerned and goes on to make all the deductions which have to be made from that amount, arriving finally at the actual net result. As an example of a typical Trading Account, let us take the figures for one month of a manufacturing business, assuming for convenience that the financial year of this business coincides with the calendar year and thus ends on December 31. The results for the month of May (the fifth month of the year) may be set out as follows.

TRADING ACCOUNT

(including Interim Profit and Loss Statement)

Month of May, 1931

	This month		Year to date		Increase (+) or Decrease (−) since	
	Amount £	%	Amount £	%	Last month £	Last year to date £
Net sales	100,000	100	450,000	100	+10,000	−150,000
Deduct Cost of Manufacturing Products sold (including depreciation of buildings, machinery, tools, etc.)	60,000	60	279,000	62	+6,000	−121,000
Gross profit	40,000	40	171,000	38	+4,000	−29,000
Deduct Selling and Distribution Expenses (including Discounts Allowed, Salesmen's Commissions, etc.)	20,000	20	94,500	21	+2,000	−25,500
Balance	20,000	20	76,500	17	+2,000	−3,500
Deduct Administrative and general Expenses	8,000	8	37,500	8·33	+1,000	−1,500
Provision for Income Tax and Bad Debts	3,000	3	13,500	3·0	−1,150	−3,000
Miscellaneous Expenses	1,000	1	3,000	·66	−350	−3,000
Net profit	8,000	8	22,500	5	+2,500	+4,000

If, as frequently happens, the company has some miscellaneous sources of income such as interest on investments, the rent derived from the lease of houses or properties, royalties on patents, etc., these would be added to the net amount received from sales before making the last of the deductions shown above, namely, the sum of the three items of the nature of general or miscellaneous charges. Income of this kind has not been included in the specimen form of Trading Account as given above in order to avoid obscuring the main issue, namely, the net income derived from the business itself.

This Trading Account will repay very careful study, for there are many very useful lessons to be learnt from it. It will be noticed that

(1) The sales for May, 1931, show an increase over those of the previous month and a still greater increase over the average monthly sales for the five months January to May inclusive. This might at first sight be taken as a clear indication that business is on the up-grade, but it is hardly ever safe to arrive at conclusions of this kind from the figures of so short a period as one month, bearing in mind that in all businesses at certain periods of the year trade is as a rule better than at others. That this is so would clearly be seen if a graph were made of the monthly sales extending over a period of years. Another fact which must always be borne in mind is that certain months of the year have fewer working days than others. This is particularly the case when during the month there happens to be a Bank Holiday or a fifth Sunday. Taking the two months under consideration, namely April and May of 1931, we shall have to bear in mind that Easter fell in April, and May had five Sundays, so that there were 26 working days in May and not more than 23 in April, that is not allowing for any dislocation of business being caused by the holiday. When due allowance is made for this it would appear that the difference in output

of the two months may be accounted for by other than trade fluctuations.

(2) The manufacturing costs and selling expenses work out at the same percentage of sales for each of the two months, but comparing May with the first five months of 1931 taken together, manufacturing costs have fallen by 2 % and selling costs by 1 %. This may be regarded as an indication of the savings that may be effected with increased output, bearing in mind that the average monthly sales for the five months was £90,000 as against the £100,000 of May.

(3) What may appear to be a comparatively slight increase in manufacturing costs may make a very considerable difference to the net income. Thus, the net income of 5 % for the five months compares very unfavourably with the 8 % for the month of May.

(4) The results for the five months, January to May, 1931, show a very considerable falling off when compared with the same period of the previous year: £450,000 against £600,000, or a decrease in sales of £150,000, that is, of 25 %.

(5) If attention is now turned to the item of manufacturing costs, it will be seen that they have been decreased to the extent of £121,000, that is to say, to £279,000 as against the previous year's figure of £400,000, or 66⅔ %. If these costs had been at the same percentage of sales for 1931 as for 1930, the difference would only have been £93,000. It is evident, therefore, that very considerable economies must have been effected during the year. This seems to be in direct contradiction to what was said at the end of (2) above, for there it was suggested that the percentage of costs to sales tended to be lower when the output was greater. Now it is the other way round: instead of there being a higher percentage of costs as the result of a very large reduction in output, the percentage is in fact lower. How is this to be accounted for?

To find an answer to this question it is necessary to consider the effect which a period of business depression is likely to have on the policy and organization of the enterprise when orders are falling off and business is becoming unprofitable. The problem which presents itself is how to reduce expenses, and so through a lower selling price to attract a larger demand. This is generally solved in two ways:

(1) By effecting economies in organization

and (2) By improving methods of production.

It may be that in the distribution of the work there is found to be a certain amount of overlapping, or the time of a highly paid worker may be occupied with some merely mechanical detail. In either case there is waste of effort and consequently unnecessary cost. To correct this, tasks will have to be redistributed, followed in many cases by a reduction in staff. Or again, an attempt is made to solve the problem by introducing new types of labour-saving machinery and by improving the lay-out of the works so as to reduce the time spent in passing the product through its various stages. In these ways much may be done to bring down costs and so to improve the competitive position of the business.

The figures given in the specimen Trading Account would suggest that this policy has been followed, and that the falling off of business has brought home the necessity of changes in organization and equipment with the result that the reduction in output has been accompanied by a reduction, not an increase, in the manufacturing costs.

(6) The result of the various economies has been that though the sales have fallen off by no less a sum than £150,000, the net amount received from the sales has only been diminished by £3500—that is, £76,500 instead of £80,000.

It may not unnaturally be asked why in this form of Trading Account the actual figures for the preceding year are not given but only the "increase or decrease". The reason is that as these accounts are rendered monthly, the directors or managers may be expected to have before them the previous returns, and hence they need to have their attention drawn only to the changes that have taken place.

The monthly Trading Account may usefully contain other information of a helpful character, such as the amount of unfilled orders that were on the books at the beginning of the month and that of the new orders received during the month, as these would be an indication of the general trend of business activity. These additional particulars may conveniently take the following form:

	1931	1930	Increase (+) or Decrease (−)
Orders on hand on May 1	150,000	200,000	−50,000
Add orders received during month	110,000	150,000	−40,000
	260,000	350,000	−90,000
Deduct orders filled during month	100,000	135,000	−35,000
Orders on hand on May 31	160,000	215,000	−55,000
Total orders received January to May	520,000	700,000	−180,000

These statistics form a useful basis of comparison and serve to indicate the general position as regards orders and output. But without explanation it would often be extremely easy to draw wrong conclusions from them. For example, the particulars just given show that the orders received during the month both in 1931 and in 1930 were considerably in excess of the orders that were actually completed. This may be due to various causes, one may be that the orders received were above the average, and that it was not thought desirable to produce at great pressure one month and to be slack the next. Another reason might be that some of the orders received during the month were for delivery in instalments as required, and hence the orders booked might show an excess over those filled. On the other hand, in the succeeding months there might be fewer orders received, but owing to the delivery of goods previously ordered, the amount compared with the heading "orders filled" might be in excess of that for "orders received"

COSTING ACCOUNTS

Here we must digress for a moment in order to consider the very important question of "Costing Accounts". In the specimen Trading Account given on p. 95 the net income, or real surplus, was arrived at after deducting from the sum obtained from the net sales three main classes of expenditure, viz. manufacturing costs, selling expenses or distributing costs, miscellaneous expenses or administrative costs. As already pointed out, when dealing with the question of account-keeping in general it is of the greatest importance that accurate accounts should be kept of the cost to the business of each unit of the product sold, and this division of costs under the three main headings is of great practical utility.

The various items covered by the inclusive term costs of production may be divided into two, direct and indirect. Direct costs are those which can be assigned to any single unit produced. Thus, in the manufacture of, say, a pair of boots, it would be quite possible to enter up the cost of the material and the cost of the labour involved in the various processes through which the material would have to pass before it became a pair of boots. These, therefore, are direct costs, and together they form what is known as the prime cost of the particular article. Indirect costs, on the other hand, are those which are incurred not for a single article but for a whole range of articles or even for the general conduct of the whole business. These are generally known as "overheads" or "oncosts". Under this heading, of course, would come all the expenses of management, the office expenses, and all out-goings for travellers, agents, advertising, etc.

The difficulty to be overcome in attempting to arrive at the complete cost of say a pair of boots of a particular size and pattern is how to determine what portion of these indirect costs should be assigned to this particular article. If all the articles made were similar it would be an easy matter to distribute these costs proportionately over the total number of articles manufactured. But this is seldom the case, and consequently some basis of distribution has to be found. The two items of direct cost, as we have already seen, are materials and labour, and the question is, therefore, would it result in the greater accuracy if the total direct cost, or if one of the two items of direct cost were taken as the basis? The argument against including materials is that the expenses of selling, of management and of administration generally, might be very much the same for each pair of boots sold whatever the material used, whereas in one pair the cost of the material might well be twice as much as in another. If then the amount of the indirect costs assigned to each pair of boots were based on a figure which included the cost of the material, the distribution of those costs would not be a fair one. Hence, the most usual course is to fall back on the other item of direct cost, namely, labour, and to add to the prime cost of each particular article a certain percentage of the wages bill to cover the expenses incurred in selling, and a certain percentage of it to cover the costs of administration. What these percentages are will depend partly on the nature of the business, for in different businesses the proportion which overheads bear to manufacturing costs may vary enormously, and partly on the scale of production, for it is well recognized that one of the chief advantages of large-scale production is that as output increases, the costs of administration do not increase in the same proportion and hence the overheads have to be distributed over a wider area.

From what has been said it is evident that Costing Accounts play a very important part in the daily business of any manufacturing concern, for they provide a record of what each particular article of manufacture costs to produce on any given scale of output, or, in other words, they provide the material for estimating the conditions of supply. These must be brought into line with the conditions of demand, and demand varies with price. Demand and supply are in the majority of cases both elastic. A lower supply price tempts a larger demand, and this calls forth a larger output, which in its turn tends to reduce cost per unit. Consequently, the manufacturer who keeps in close touch with the conditions of demand, and thus knows what price he must work to, is able through his costing accounts to estimate what his output must be to enable him to sell his goods at a profit. His efforts are necessarily directed towards effecting a reduction in production costs, and for this he looks, apart from a closer co-ordination of labour and capital and improved industrial appliances, to his being able to distribute his overhead costs over a larger area of output.

DEPRECIATION

Before leaving the subject of Costing Accounts it is necessary to say something about the question of "Depreciation". It will be noticed that in the specimen Trading Account given earlier in this chapter, Depreciation was included under the heading of "Cost of Manufacturing Products sold". This, however, is not the universal practice, for we often find that the "Profit on Trading", as shown in the Profit and Loss Account, is arrived at before any deduction for Depreciation has been made, and that the allowance for Depreciation is included among the miscellaneous items deducted from that "Profit on Trading" before arriving at the "Net Profit".

There is a very strong argument in favour of adopting the

practice here followed, viz. that of regarding Depreciation as one of the Manufacturing Costs. There are two kinds of capital employed in the manufacture of any commodity:

(1) Circulating capital, such as raw material, which can only perform its function once.

(2) Fixed capital, such as buildings, plant, machinery and tools, which can perform its function continuously for a longer or shorter period of time.

It would be conceded by all that replacement of capital has to be made out of the product of the industry, and that this replacement is twofold, viz. the whole of the value of the circulating capital used up for each unit of manufacture, and such a portion of the value of the fixed capital employed as will replace such capital when it wears out or becomes obsolete.

It is surely then logical to regard both of these as being of the nature of manufacturing costs, the one direct and the other indirect, and as such in the Trading Account to include both alike in the first deduction from the amount of "Net Sales".

CHAPTER VIII

READING THE BALANCE SHEET

Annual Balance Sheet and Profit and Loss Account

We now come to the other two forms of financial statement, viz. the Balance Sheet and the Profit and Loss Account. It is from these two statements that the proprietors of the business—whether they are the partners of a private firm or the shareholders of a public company—are able to obtain definite information as to the results of the year's trading and the general financial position of the undertaking. In the case of a public company the Companies Act of 1929 lays down very strict regulations as to the publication of the accounts and as to the contents of the balance sheet. The relevant sections of the Act are here quoted in order that the reader may have before him the legal requirements with regard to this matter.[1]

123. (1) The directors of every company shall at some date not later than eighteen months after the incorporation of the company and subsequently once at least in every calendar year lay before the company in general meeting a profit and loss account or, in the case of a company not trading for profit, an income and expenditure account for the period, in the case of the first account, since the incorporation of the company, and, in any other case, since the preceding account, made up to a date not earlier than the date of the meeting by more than nine months, or, in the case of a company carrying on business or having interests abroad, by more than twelve months.

(2) The directors shall cause to be made out in every calendar year, and to be laid before the company in general meeting, a balance sheet as at the date to which the profit and loss account, or the income and expenditure account, as the case may be, is made up, and there shall be attached to every such balance sheet a report

[1] Companies Act, 1929, Sections 123, 124.

by the directors with respect to the state of the company's affairs, the amount, if any, which they recommend should be paid by way of dividend, and the amount, if any, which they propose to carry to the reserve fund, general reserve or reserve account shown specifically on the balance sheet, or to a reserve fund, general reserve or reserve account to be shown specifically on a subsequent balance sheet.

124. (1) Every balance sheet of a company shall contain a summary of the authorized share capital and of the issued share capital of the company, its liabilities and its assets, together with such particulars as are necessary to disclose the general nature of the liabilities and the assets of the company and to distinguish between the amounts respectively of the fixed assets and of the floating assets, and shall state how the values of the fixed assets have been arrived at.

I. THE BALANCE SHEET

The use of the term "balance" in connection with the keeping of accounts is borrowed from the weighing machine, the two sides of which must balance one another, that is to say, must be in a state of equilibrium.

The word "balance" itself is derived from the Latin *bis*, "double", and *lanx*, "a dish". Hence a balance is literally a pair of dishes or scales. In a pair of scales we have the goods to be weighed on one side, and the standard weights on the other. When the two exactly balance one another we are able to say what the weight of the goods in question is. Similarly, with the annual account known as the Balance Sheet we have the Liabilities of the company on the one side and its Assets on the other, and the two sides when added up are made to correspond by the addition to whichever side requires it of the amount of which it happens to fall short, or, in other words, of the balance.

This draws our attention to the two uses that are made of the term "Balance":

(1) In the "Balance Sheet" we have the statement which exhibits the two sides in equilibrium.

(2) In the "Balance" we have the difference between the two sides of an account, i.e. what is necessary to make the two sides equal and so bring about the equilibrium.

For anyone unaccustomed to handle such matters the reading of a Balance Sheet may well seem to present almost insuperable difficulties. With a little explanation, however, the task should not be by any means an impossible one. As already pointed out, its purpose is to give the shareholders such information about the Assets and Liabilities of the company as will enable them to judge its true financial position. For this two things are essential, the Balance Sheet must be clear and it must be complete: that is to say, the items must be set out in such a way as to leave no double as to the real nature of each, and the items taken together must cover, though not necessarily give details of, the whole of the company's financial affairs. At the same time it should be borne in mind that a Balance Sheet is not an account in itself, but a grouping together of several accounts so as to show in a condensed form the actual financial position at a glance.

In drawing up the Balance Sheet it is the practice in this country to place the Liabilities on the left-hand or Debit side and the Assets on the right-hand or Credit side, the company being regarded as a debtor for everything it has received and for what it owes, and as a creditor for every use it has made of the money entrusted to it as well as for all amounts due to it but not yet paid. In some continental and other countries the order is reversed, the Assets being placed on the left-hand side and the Liabilities on the right, while in others it is not unusual to set out the Assets vertically over the Liabilities or vice versa.

In the specimen Balance Sheet given below the balance of profit is necessarily shown on the "Liabilities" side and as such represents a part of the company's liability to its shareholders, but had there been a loss the amount of such a loss would in order to balance have to appear under "Assets".

A loss appearing as an asset is obviously a misnomer and it is now customary among the leading Chartered Accountants and Public Auditors to leave out altogether the words Assets and Liabilities as a heading for the Balance Sheet. They are included here only because it affords a clearer understanding of the foregoing and subsequent remarks.

The first thing to be entered on the "Liabilities" side is the amount received from the shareholders by way of subscription to the company's capital, and on the "Assets" side how the money so received has been expended or otherwise made use of. As the business of the company develops there will have to be additional sums entered on the "Liabilities" side as having been borrowed or otherwise placed at the company's disposal and there will have to be corresponding entries on the "Assets" side, accounting for how these sums too have been utilized. The essence of the whole thing is that the Balance Sheet has to show

(1) How the moneys entrusted to the company have been used, or, in other words, what form those moneys now take.

(2) Whether at the end of the financial year the company is better or worse off than it was at the beginning.

The construction of the Balance Sheet can be conveniently explained by showing how it is gradually built up, stage by stage, from the beginning of the company's existence.

Stage I

Let us suppose that a company has just been floated with a capital of £500,000 in ordinary shares of £1 each. The issue has been fully subscribed and the shares have all been paid for in full, the money so received having been deposited with the company's bankers.

The company has not yet commenced operations, so a Balance Sheet drawn up at this stage would take very much the following form:

BALANCE SHEET

LIABILITIES	£	s.	d.	£	s.	d.
Authorized Capital						
500,000 Ordinary Shares of £1 each	500,000	0	0			
Issued Capital						
500,000 Ordinary Shares of £1 each, fully paid				500,000	0	0
				£500,000	0	0

It is probable that many of the applications for shares would have been made on behalf of their clients by bankers or stockbrokers who would be entitled to deduct a small commission. There might also have been certain other "Preliminary Expenses" connected with the promotion or flotation of the company. In such cases the sum given as "Cash at Bank" would be less than £500,000 by the amount of such Commission or Preliminary Expenses—say £15,000—and this would have to be shown in the Balance Sheet, the Assets side thus standing:

Cash at Bank	£485,000
Commission on applications and other Preliminary Expenses	£15,000
	£500,000

Stage II

The company having commenced trading, we may assume that goods have been manufactured and sold, and that the expenses of production have been met by the sums received from the sale of the goods. But when the books are closed at the end of the year and the Balance Sheet is drawn up, there are certain to be various amounts still owing by the company for purchases of different kinds as well as some owing to the company by its customers. The former will then appear on the side of "Liabilities" under the heading of "Sundry

AS AT...... 193...

ASSETS	£	s.	d.
Cash at Bank	500,000	0	0
	£500,000	0	0

Creditors" and the latter on that of "Assets" under the heading of "Sundry Debtors".

By this time the sum of £500,000, originally entered as "Cash at Bank", has been further diminished by the expenses incurred in connection with the purchase of a suitable site, the erection of the necessary buildings and the installation of machinery and power-plant. These items will duly appear on the "Assets" side; they are merely a portion of the capital of the company in another form.

Though the costs incurred in manufacturing are expected to be recovered out of the price for which the goods are sold, these costs have to be incurred in advance. Wages have to be paid week by week and salaries month by month. Raw material has to be bought and bills have to be paid for fuel and stores of various kinds. Rent, rates and other current expenses have to be met. For all these various purposes money has to be found, and another part of the "Cash at Bank" has now found its way into "Stocks on hand", a heading which may be taken to cover stocks of raw material and of finished and partly finished goods, as well as of all sorts of stores.

It very often happens that the company has not sufficient working capital to pay out so much money in advance and so it has recourse to its bankers, who are asked for a loan or a credit in the form of an overdraft, that is, as explained later on, the right to draw cheques up to a certain

BALANCE SHEET

December 31,

LIABILITIES	£	s.	d.	£	s.	d.
Authorized Capital						
500,000 Ordinary Shares of £1 each	500,000	0	0			
Issued Capital						
500,000 Ordinary Shares of £1 each, fully paid				500,000	0	0
Bank Loan				20,000	0	0
Sundry Creditors				30,000	0	0
Balance from Profit and Loss Account				50,250	0	0
				£600,250	0	0

amount in excess of what it has at the time standing to its credit in the books of the bank. As this overdraft places an additional sum of money at the disposal of the company, it must be entered on the "Liabilities" side, and its corresponding entry on the other side of the account must be looked for either in the sum due from the "Sundry Debtors" for goods delivered but not yet paid for, or in that part of "Stocks on hand" which represents goods which have been made to order but which have not yet been delivered, from both of which sources money can be expected to be coming in shortly.

At the end of the first year's trading, then, the Balance Sheet would probably contain all the various entries suggested above and would be somewhat in the form given above.

The only item which has so far not been explained is the last one on the "Liabilities" side, viz. "Balance from Profit and Loss Account, £50,250". Without this entry the assets would have exceeded the liabilities by this amount, thus showing that during the year the position of the company had improved to that extent.

To account for the £50,250 we must look at the Profit and Loss Account which would have been distributed to all the shareholders, together with the Directors' Report and the

FOR THE YEAR ENDED

1931

Assets	£	s.	d.	£	s.	d.
Cash in hand and in Current Account at Bank				1,250	0	0
Buildings, Machinery, Plant, and Office furniture and equipment, at cost, less Depreciation				360,000	0	0
Stocks on hand				170,000	0	0
Sundry Debtors	75,000	0	0			
less Reserve against Bad and Doubtful Debts	6,000	0	0			
				69,000	0	0
				£600,250	0	0

Balance Sheet, when sending out the notice of the Annual General Meeting at which the accounts would be submitted for the shareholders' approval.

II. THE PROFIT AND LOSS ACCOUNT

The first thing to consider is how the Profit and Loss Account is drawn up. Some companies present this account to the shareholders in a very concentrated form, merely showing on the debit side a single amount covering all the various items of expenditure, and on the credit side also a single amount representing the whole of the company's income whether derived from sales or from other sources of revenue. If income exceeds expenditure, the difference is shown as "Profit" and appears as such on the Liabilities side of the Balance Sheet. If, on the other hand, expenditure exceeds income, the difference is entered as "Loss" and appears as such on the Assets side of the Balance Sheet.

It should be noted that under the Companies Act of 1929, the amounts paid to directors by way of remuneration for their services must always be shown as a separate item.[1]

[1] Companies Act, 1929, Section 128.

A Profit and Loss Account of this type would take very much the following form:

PROFIT AND LOSS ACCOUNT
for the year ended......

Dr.	£	s.	d.		£	s.	d. Cr.
To Manufacturing and Selling Costs (including Depreciation), Interest and Administrative Expenses	90,000	o	o	By Sales, Commissions, Interest, etc. ...	100,000	o	o
Directors' remuneration ...	1,000	o	o				
Net Profit carried to Balance Sheet	9,000	o	o				
	£100,000	o	o		£100,000	o	o

Another form of Profit and Loss Account, and one more generally adopted than the foregoing, gives no figures for the income derived from sales, etc., or for that part of the expenditure which consists of manufacturing and selling costs. In their place we have:

(1) On the right-hand side:

(a) Profit on trading, which, as shown in the specimen Trading Account given on p. 95, is what remains of the amount received from net sales after the manufacturing costs (including Depreciation), selling expenses, and such of the administrative expenses as were not shown separately on the left-hand side of the Profit and Loss Account, have been deducted.

(b) Any other forms of income, such as that which may be derived from investments, or that which is obtained by way of commission or interest, are shown as separate items.

(2) On the left-hand side are set out one under the other:

(a) Certain miscellaneous expenses which are incurred in the general administration of the business and which it is usual or obligatory to set out separately, such as directors' fees, the interest which has to be paid on bank overdraft or advances, and auditors' fees.

(*b*) Interest on Debenture Stock, if any such has been issued.

On the assumption that the Profit and Loss Account which according to law would have accompanied the Balance Sheet given on pp. 110–11 was of this latter type, we may take it that it would probably have been very much in the following form:

PROFIT AND LOSS ACCOUNT

for the year ended December 31, 1931

Dr.					Cr.
	£	s. d.		£	s. d.
To Directors' Fees... ...	1,000	0 0	By Profit on Trading ...	52,000	0 0
Bank Interest and charges	500	0 0			
Auditors' Fees	250	0 0			
Net Profit carried to Balance Sheet	50,250	0 0			
	£52,000	0 0		£52,000	0 0

Here it will be seen that the "Profit on Trading" of £52,000 was diminished by certain payments amounting in all to £1750, the effect of which was to leave a Net Profit of £50,250.

In the Report, which under the Companies Act the Directors have to issue to the shareholders, it has to be stated how it is proposed to deal with the Net Profit. It may be that for this particular year the profit happens to be a small one, in which case no part of it would be distributed to the shareholders by way of dividend, but the whole amount would be regarded as a necessary balance in hand and would be "carried forward" to the next account. But in the specimen account just given, the profit is sufficiently large to justify the payment of a dividend as well as the making of some provision for the strengthening of the company's financial position by placing a portion of it to "Reserve".

The Article in Table A[1] which deals with the question of Reserves is as follows:

Article 93. The Directors may, before recommending any dividend, set aside out of the profits of the company such sums as they think proper as a reserve or reserves which shall, at the discretion of the Directors, be applicable for meeting contingencies, or for equalizing dividends, or for any other purpose to which the profits of the company may be properly applied, and pending such application may, at the like discretion, either be employed in the business of the company or be invested in such investments (other than shares of the company) as the Directors may from time to time think fit.

The "Reserve" may be general and used for any purpose for which it may be required, or it may be "special", that is, earmarked for some particular purpose such as payment of Income Tax, or making provision against some specific contingency.

The "Appropriation", as it is called, of the £50,250 which in the above Profit and Loss Account was shown as Net Profit, may be set out as follows:

	£
To General Reserve	15,000
To Dividend on the Share Capital at 5% per annum	25,000
To be carried forward	10,250
	£50,250

THE BALANCE SHEET. FINAL FORM

In the Balance Sheets of the second and following years, we have to enter the amount placed to Reserve and the Balance brought forward from the preceding one, and at the same time make clear any changes in the position that have taken place during the financial year under review.

There is no prescribed form which the Balance Sheet is bound to follow. All that is necessary is that the requirements of the Companies Act as quoted above should be complied

[1] For the Articles of Association see Chapter v, p. 66.

BALANCE SHEET FOR THE YEAR ENDED

December 31, 1932

	£	s.	d.	£	s.	d.	£	s.	d.
CAPITAL LIABILITIES									
Authorized									
500,000 Ordinary Shares of £1 each	500,000	0	0						
Issued and fully paid									
500,000 Ordinary Shares of £1 each				500,000	0	0			
Reserves									
General Reserve				15,000	0	0			
CURRENT LIABILITIES									
Bank Loan	25,000	0	0						
Sundry Creditors and Bills Payable	35,000	0	0	60,000	0	0			
PROFIT AND LOSS ACCOUNT									
Balance brought forward from 1931	10,250	0	0						
Profit for the year	23,250	0	0	33,500	0	0			
				£608,500	0	0			

	£	s.	d.	£	s.	d.
CAPITAL ASSETS						
Buildings, Machinery and Plant, also Office furniture and equipment, at cost, less Depreciation				330,000	0	0
CURRENT ASSETS						
Cash in hand and at Bank	1,500	0	0			
Sundry Debtors (less Reserve against bad debts) and Bills Receivable	82,000	0	0			
Stocks on hand	195,000	0	0	278,500	0	0
				£608,500	0	0

with. Hence, though the Balance Sheets of different companies may and do differ in arrangement, the general features remain the same.

The form here adopted may be regarded as typical of a great many and it has the advantage of avoiding unnecessary complications. It is now given in its final stage, showing how the net result of the previous year's trading is dealt with and arranging the items in groups for convenience of analysis and study.

The Profit and Loss Account which would have accompanied this second year's Balance Sheet would doubtless have been exactly similar in form to that for 1931, a copy of which was given on p. 113. This year the Net Profit carried forward to the Balance Sheet is only £23,250, and this with the £10,250 brought forward from the previous year gives a distributable amount of £33,500. Under these circumstances it is evident that the Appropriation cannot be on the same scale as on the former occasion. If it were decided to maintain the dividend at 5 %, there would not be enough left over to add something more to the Reserve Fund and at the same time to carry forward to next year what might be considered as a suitable amount. Hence the former would probably be omitted, in which case the Appropriation might be as follows:

To Dividend on the Share Capital at 5 % per annum	£25,000
To be carried forward	£8,500
	£33,500

It would, however, under the circumstances be more prudent either to forgo the dividend altogether—to pass the dividend is the usual way of expressing it—or to pay a smaller dividend, say 4 %, and place the £5000 thus saved to "General Reserve", leaving the carry forward at £8500.

READING THE BALANCE SHEET

When the accounts are published the shareholders naturally look first at the Profit and Loss Account, for in that they can see at a glance how the company's business has prospered during the past year. This is of very great importance to them, for it is only when profits are made that they can expect to receive dividends on the capital they have invested in the concern.

Their study of the accounts must not, however, end here, for it is quite possible for the Profit and Loss Account to show quite a considerable balance on the right side, based on the original valuation of the Assets, and yet for the company's financial position to be worse at the end of the year than it was at the beginning. There may have been a gain in trading but at the same time there may have been what are called "capital" losses. For example, the company's investments may have fallen in value, its stocks of finished goods may have become almost worthless owing perhaps to some change of fashion or to a cheaper substitute having been found. A building, insufficiently insured, may have suffered from fire, flood or riot. A dishonest official may have falsified the accounts and under cover of this have robbed the company.

With these possibilities the original surplus would, through the writing down of the stocks or investments to their actual value, or the diminution of the value of properties, etc., have shrunk to nothing or even have been converted into a loss.

Shareholders who are really interested in the business itself will want to compare each Balance Sheet presented to them with those of previous years in order to form an idea as to whether the general tendency is an upward or downward one. They will be keen to note any changes that have taken place in the indebtedness of the company or in the value and character of its Assets.

Two very important questions to which the Balance Sheet may be expected to provide the answers are:

(1) Is the company prosperous or the reverse?

(2) Is the company's position sufficiently liquid?

Let us examine the specimen Balance Sheet given on p. 115 and see what can be learnt from it in both these matters.

I. *The General Position*

The first thing we shall notice is that the Assets are £33,500 more than the Liabilities and that the sums brought from the Profit and Loss Account, which enable both sides to balance, represent the net profit made during the year under review, £23,250, and the balance carried forward after the previous year's appropriation, £10,250. This result is not so good as that formerly shown, but still it indicates that the company continues to work at a profit.

But the question we are here bound to ask is—"Are the various assets worth the sums assigned to them?" That is to say, "Are the Buildings and other Capital Assets overvalued? Are the Stocks overvalued? Are the finished goods included under the heading 'Stocks' really saleable and likely to be turned into cash within a reasonable time? Do they represent a larger quantity of goods in proportion to the volume of sales than is usual in this particular class of business?"

It is on the answers to these questions that the whole matter rests, and it is because the ordinary shareholder has no means of getting at the real facts that he not infrequently forms a very erroneous impression of the general position.

The Balance Sheet has in fact to be very largely taken on trust: trust in the Board of Directors who have presented the accounts, and trust in the Auditors who have certified them. The figures correspond with those in the company's books. The fixed assets are as a rule entered "at cost less depreciation", and the stocks at a figure which has been written down to what may be regarded as the actual current value. This is how we may assume the figures given in our specimen Balance Sheet have been arrived at, and thus, provided that the original cost of the fixed assets was not excessive and that they are really suited to the purposes of the business, we may regard the surplus shown as genuinely representing the profits of the year.

II. The Liquid Position

To arrive at the Liquid Position we must compare the Current Assets with the Current Liabilities, that is to say, we must set what the company has in cash, or convertible into cash, against what it owes to the Bank or to other creditors. This calculation will give us what is known as the "working capital". Assuming that sufficient allowance has been made for bad or doubtful debts, it would appear from our Balance Sheet that, in addition to the £1500 in cash, the company can reckon on getting in £22,000, the difference between the Sundry Debtors and the Current Liabilities. This would appear to be a reasonably liquid position, but this position would be improved if, as might well be the case, there happened to be a larger stock of finished goods than it was really necessary to carry and the surplus were sold without subsequent replacement of stock. It might happen also that the company possessed certain short-term investments, or securities readily disposed of on the Stock Exchange. If either of these figured in the Balance Sheet, they would have to be taken into account in estimating the company's liquid position.

DEBENTURES AND RESERVES

Besides "Issued Capital" one not infrequently sees in a Balance Sheet that the company has made an issue of "Debentures". Debentures differ from Share Capital inasmuch as to them is attached a definite undertaking of repayment. They bear a fixed rate of interest, which must be paid before any dividends can be declared, and they are often secured by a mortgage on the fixed assets of the company. They are therefore in reality of the nature of a long-period loan, and this must be taken into account when forming an estimate of the general position.

Reserves on the other hand, though also appearing on the Liabilities side, are a source of strength to a company. They give the shareholders confidence that should emergencies arise provision has been made for meeting them, and that, if owing to trade fluctuations profits should diminish or even fall off altogether, there would be a fund out of which dividends could be maintained or solvency preserved until better times come round again. It should, however, be pointed out that if the company's Assets had been overvalued, the Reserves shown would in reality, in whole or in part, be fictitious, and hence in such a case they could not be regarded as strengthening the company's financial position.

CHAPTER IX

THE DEVELOPMENT OF THE BANKING SYSTEM

It was pointed out in the opening chapter of this book that the very essence of economic life is the interchange of services between the members of a community, and in a still wider sense between people living in all the different parts of the world. In very early times this interchange took the form of bartering service for service or commodity for commodity, but that system soon gave place to one in which there was an accepted medium of exchange, and under modern conditions this medium takes the form of currency or credit instruments. In the business world the term money is used to cover both of these, inasmuch as it embraces not merely the coin or notes which form the currency but also all other means of effecting payments, such as cheques and bills of exchange.

In all countries where trade is at all highly developed some machinery has to be set up for carrying out the process of exchange. Buyer and seller are, except in the case of retail trade, for the most part at a distance from one another and have no personal touch with one another: they may even be in different countries and different hemispheres. It is to supply this machinery that banks mainly exist.

In business life the bank is the very centre of all commercial activity. No business can go on without it. It is through the banks that the currency of the country is kept circulating and in this way is enabled to discharge satisfactorily its function of being given and received in exchange for goods and services. It is through the banks and the cheque system which has arisen in connection with them that debts can be discharged by means of book entries without any use of currency at all. It is through the banks, though in a somewhat different way, that it is possible to carry on foreign trade by setting the indebtedness of people in one country against the indebtedness of people in another. And, again, it is through the banks that advances are made to manufacturers and merchants, enabling them to undertake business for which their cash position at the moment is not sufficiently strong.

The banking system of to-day is the outcome of a long period of development and of adaptation to changing economic conditions and to the ever-growing complexity of life in the business world. Its development has been a gradual one. All banks were not established to meet the same financial need or to exercise the same business function. For example, some of the early Italian banks, of which perhaps the Bank of St George at Genoa, founded in 1407, is a very good example, were formed more as finance companies to make loans to their various Governments. Their operations extended, too, far outside the State in which they were established. As merchants they carried on trade in distant countries, and as financiers they acted as money-lenders not only to their own ruling houses but also to monarchs like our own Edward I and Edward III, whose wars made it difficult for them to make their revenue sufficient to meet their expenditure. Another important and very profitable business for them was that of acting as Papal Agents, collecting in the different countries of Europe and remitting to Rome the Papal revenues which were derived from bishopric, monastery or benefice.

The Bank of Amsterdam was founded for a very different purpose. The extensive foreign trade carried on by the Dutch brought into Holland currencies of many different countries, and these varied greatly not merely in denomination but also in quality. Hence, in Holland there were in circulation at the same time all kinds of coins, some of which were low in

standard, some debased, some worn or clipped, as well as the
newly coined money of good value issued from the Amsterdam mint. This placed many difficulties in the way of
business. Merchants might be quite adequately supplied
with coined money with which to make their purchases, but
it was not always easy to get the sellers of the goods to take
in payment a miscellaneous collection of coins of which they
could not judge the intrinsic worth. In these circumstances
it will be readily understood that the so-called "Gresham's
Law"[1] came into operation and that the bad money drove out
the good. Hence, almost as soon as it was issued, the good
Dutch money ran the risk of being melted down or exported,
leaving only coins of poorer quality in circulation and a state
of the currency growing progressively worse.

Uncertainty as to the value of such a mixed currency as
has just been described led to a natural disinclination on the
part of foreign traders to accept money from Holland and
hence, when foreign bills of exchange drawn on Amsterdam
were presented for payment in that city, it not infrequently
happened that the money tendered was at a considerable
discount.

It was to remedy situations such as these that the Bank of
Amsterdam was founded in 1609. Into it all the various types
of money could be paid and merchants would receive in
return what was called "bank money", that is, a credit in the
books of the Bank to the amount in good standard Dutch
currency of the intrinsic value of the coins deposited, less a
small charge for the expenses connected with re-coinage and
management. At the same time a law was passed that all bills
of 600 guilders and upwards drawn at Amsterdam, or negotiated there, should be paid in the new bank money, and hence
it became necessary for all merchants to keep an account with
the Bank, for otherwise they would not have been able to

[1] Some account of Sir Thomas Gresham is given in Chapter xiv in
the section dealing with the Royal Exchange.

meet their obligations. As therefore the bank money represented coin of full standard value, bills of exchange could at all times be considered as worth the full amount written on them, and as a consequence the rate of exchange soon ceased to be unfavourable. This again tended to raise the credit of Amsterdam as a financial centre and to appreciate the value of its currency in other countries. The advantages of this Dutch bank money are summed up by Adam Smith in the following words:

Bank money over and above its intrinsic superiority to currency, and the additional value which this demand necessarily gives it, has likewise some other advantages. It is secure from fire, robbery, and other accidents; the City of Amsterdam is bound for it; it can be paid away by a simple transfer, without the trouble of counting, or the risk of transporting it from one place to another.[1]

A banking experiment of another kind was made for the first time in Sweden. The first bank to be founded in that country obtained its charter in 1656. It consisted of two separate departments—the deposit or current account bank, taking charge of the money of its customers and issuing it to them as and when they required it, and a "loan bank" whose business it was to make advances against real property and other forms of tangible wealth. Some five years later, that is in 1661, this bank commenced an issue of bank notes or paper money. This is generally regarded as being the first use of this form of circulating medium. The recklessness, however, with which the notes were issued soon brought the bank to ruin, and in 1668, in order to save the situation, a State Bank, with the name "Estates of the Realm Bank", to be known later as the Bank of Sweden, was established in its place. This bank was to be under the management of the Estates of the Realm, the Parliament of that day, the intention being to place it in a position entirely independent of royal control. The business of the bank was to be carried on on very much

<hr>

[1] Adam Smith, *Wealth of Nations*, Book IV, Chap. III.

the same lines as those followed by the earlier bank, but with a notable exception, namely, that the issue of bank notes was prohibited, and this was not again permitted until 1701.

THE BANK OF ENGLAND

English banking may be said to date from the foundation of the Bank of England in 1694. The circumstances which led to this very important event are well worth recalling. In the Middle Ages, owing to the laws against usury, money-lending for interest was not an occupation that Englishmen could take up. Until their expulsion from England in 1290 the Jews discharged the function of money-lenders, and when they left their place was taken to a large extent by merchants from the larger Italian cities to whom some reference has already been made. After the Reformation, however, there was a considerable change in the attitude of people in general towards this question of interest, and already in the early seventeenth century we find that money-lending has become a recognized part of the business of the goldsmiths. Money and other valuables were frequently deposited with them, sometimes merely for safe keeping, but often also as security against loans. On some of these deposits the goldsmiths would themselves pay interest, and they could well afford to do so for they demanded a higher rate from those who borrowed these same funds from them. Like a modern bank of deposit, therefore, they received deposits on which they paid interest and they made advances against security for trade and other purposes. Charles II borrowed freely from them, but when in 1672 he announced that though he would continue to pay interest he did not intend to repay the capital— the so-called "Stop of the Exchequer"—the system of borrowing from the goldsmiths received a somewhat serious blow.

The Stuarts had borrowed from the goldsmiths in anticipation of revenue, giving them as a rule the security of the taxes for their loans, but the wars of William III forced the Government to borrow on a scale that was not only beyond both the willingness and the capacity of the goldsmiths to finance, but was also beyond the possibility of repayment out of revenue. It was at this juncture that William Paterson came forward with his scheme for a Bank of England—a joint stock concern with a capital of £1,200,000. The whole of this capital was to be lent to the Government without any specified conditions of repayment, and in return the Bank was to receive an annual payment of £100,000 as interest, which amount was really 8 % on the money advanced together with a sum of £4000 for management. Thus the founding of the Bank of England is associated with the beginning of the English National Debt.

By the time the Bank was founded, the main functions of a bank were all fairly well understood and were being practised in one way or another. The four chief of these functions may be enumerated as being:

(1) The issue of paper money.
(2) The receiving of deposits from customers and returning them as and when required.
(3) The making of advances to industry and trade.
(4) The discounting of bills.

It was only the first of these which was new in England, for the three other functions had all been discharged by the goldsmiths. The right to issue paper money was included in the Bank's Charter of Incorporation. The £100,000 paid annually by the Government was originally the basis of this paper issue which the Bank was authorized to make to the extent of the amount which had been lent to the Government.

It is this issue of paper money which differentiates most clearly the Bank of England from those business undertakings in the City of London which, as has already been pointed out, had for some time exercised the banking functions of re-

ceiving deposits and granting loans. The power of the goldsmiths to lend was limited naturally by what had actually been
deposited with them. The Bank, on the other hand, could
issue paper money to a larger amount than its deposits, re-
taining only what its directors regarded as an adequate reserve. Thus a new type of money was put into circulation,
depending for its value on confidence in the prudent administration of the issuing bank and in its power to convert
its notes into coin on demand.

At the time of the English Revolution of 1689, the coinage
of the country was in a very bad state. The clipping of coins
had become a regular practice and there was a considerable
amount of base money in circulation. To quote from a tract
that attracted much attention at the time:

Great contentions do daily arise among the King's Subjects in
Fairs, Markets, Shops and other Places throughout the Kingdom
about the Passing or Refusing of the Same, to the disturbance of
the Public Peace; many Bargains, Doings and Dealings are totally
prevented and laid aside, which lessens Trade in general; Persons
before they conclude in any Bargains, are necessitated first to
settle the Price or Value of the very Money they are to Receive for
their Goods; and if it be in Guineas at a High Rate, or in Clipt or
Bad Moneys, they set the Price of their Goods accordingly which
I think has been One great cause of Raising the Price not only of
merchandizes, but even of Edibles, and other Necessaries for the
sustenance of the Common People, to their Great Grievance. The
receipt and collection of the Publick Taxes, Revenues and Debts
(as well as of Private Mens Incomes) are extreamly retarded.[1]

To remedy this state of things it was decided in 1696 to
have a complete re-coinage. This involved the calling in of
all the coins in circulation and the issue of new money of a
standard weight and fineness. During the process, however,
there was naturally a very considerable shortage of coin and
this afforded an opportunity for its rivals to make an attack
on the Bank. The goldsmiths proceeded to collect a very large

[1] W. Lowndes, *Essay for the Amendment of the Gold and Silver Coins*
(1695). Quoted by Dr W. Cunningham.

number of the Bank's notes and then presented them for immediate payment. This amounted in fact to what we should now call a "run on the Bank". In spite of this the Bank continued to meet the demands upon it which arose in the ordinary course of trade, and when the shareholders came to the rescue by putting up more money, the directors succeeded in getting safely through the crisis.

The strength of the Bank's position lay in the main in two very clear advantages which it possessed:

(1) Its connection with the Government.

(2) Its monopolistic position.

Like the early Italian banks it was the needs of the State which brought the Bank of England into existence and not only did it make advances to the Government but it acted as the Government's bankers as well. The money received from the taxes was deposited with the Bank and from that account such amounts were drawn out from time to time as were needed to meet the public expenditure. As the latter were often considerably more than the former it involved fresh loans, and thus the credit of the State affected the credit of the Bank while the amount of business arising from the connection added greatly to the Bank's wealth and importance, which were still further increased when in 1751 the Bank took over the management of the National Debt.

A clause in the Act of 1697 conferred on the Bank the privilege of being the sole Joint Stock Bank with the right to issue notes and this was always considered to give the Bank a monopoly of Joint Stock banking. For more than a century, therefore, no other Joint Stock Bank existed, all other banks being private banks. There were, however, many of these private banks all over the country and they were in the habit of issuing their own notes. But as willingness to accept bank notes other than those which were legal tender, that is other than those of the Bank of England, would depend on the confidence in the issuer, it follows that the area of circulation of the notes of these private banks would be more or less limited to the district in which the principals of the banks resided and were known. The assumed right of the Bank of England to be the sole Joint Stock Bank was withdrawn in 1826 by an Act authorizing the establishment of Joint Stock Banks outside a radius of sixty-five miles from London, and in 1833, when the Charter of the Bank of England was renewed, it was made clear that no monopoly of Joint Stock banking was conferred even in the London area, but the provision was inserted that no Joint Stock Bank within the sixty-five mile limit should have the right to issue bank notes.

THE BANK CHARTER ACT OF 1844[1]

The Bank of England's Charter came up again for renewal in 1844, and Parliament took advantage of this in passing the Bank Charter Act of that year to effect a very considerable re-organization of banking methods, the lines of which have been followed to the present day. One great departure, however, from the provisions of that Act was made in the Gold Standard Act of 1925, which did away with the convertibility of the Bank's notes by enacting that "The Bank of England shall not be bound to pay any note of the Bank in legal coin".

The Bank Charter Act of 1844 is of sufficient importance to justify a somewhat lengthy explanation of its provisions, for without a clear grasp of the scheme which then became law, and of the amendments of that law which have since been made, it would be impossible to understand fully the banking system as it exists at the present day.

In the first place the operations of the Bank were to be carried on in two distinct departments working independently of one another: the Issue Department, which was to concern

[1] "An Act to regulate the Issue of Bank Notes and for giving to the Governor and Company of the Bank of England certain Privileges for a limited Period."

itself solely with the issue of bank notes and their redemption on demand, and the Banking Department, which was to carry on the ordinary business of a bank receiving deposits, making advances and discounting bills of exchange.

The relation which was to exist between the total note issue and the gold reserve in the cellars of the Bank was strictly defined. Notes to the value of £14,000,000 were allowed to be issued without gold reserve, the security for these being £11,000,000 in Government Stock, representing the amount that the Government had borrowed from the Bank, and £3,000,000 in other securities. All issue of notes in excess of this amount was to be covered by gold or bullion in the vaults of the Issue Department. The "authorized issue", as that portion of the issue not covered by gold was designated, was allowed to be augmented from time to time to the extent of two-thirds of the issues of such other note-issuing banks as ceased to issue bank notes. In 1914 the total amount of the authorized issue was 18½ millions. After the war, by which time all other issues had ceased, it reached the amount of 19¾ millions, at which figure it remained until the whole system of note issue was changed by the Currency and Bank Notes Act of 1928.

Another very important provision of the Act of 1844 was that which obliged the Bank to purchase all gold bullion brought to it at £3. 17s. 9d. per ounce. The notes issued were all convertible into gold on demand, and thus the amount of the notes issued regulated itself automatically; when gold came in, notes went out in payment for it, and when the notes were brought back gold went out in exchange for them, and the notes so redeemed were destroyed. Hence the note issue at any time was kept equal to the gold reserve plus the authorized issue.

Other provisions included the forbidding of any banks which were not issuing notes prior to May, 1844, to issue their own notes, and of all banks already issuing notes to increase the amount of their normal issue. The absorption of country note-issuing banks by larger institutions has led to the gradual extinction of the so-called "country notes", with the result that what half a century ago were private banking institutions have now for the most part become branches of one or other of the "Big Five".

To the Act of 1844 was attached a schedule giving the form in which weekly reports of the Bank were to be made, and this form is still in use. Every Thursday morning the directors of the Bank of England meet and issue a report as to the state of the note issue and as to the current position of the Banking Department.

CHANGES SINCE 1844

The Act of 1844 remained unaltered until 1914, when the situation created by the outbreak of war led to certain changes being made. At that time the Bank of England note was, with the exception of the small number of country notes still being issued, the only form of paper currency in use, and no English note was of less value than £5. On the outbreak of war, however, it was decided to "authorize the issue of Currency Notes and to make provision with respect to the note issues of banks". This was made law by the "Currency and Bank Notes Act" of 1914, of which the following is the principal clause:

The Treasury may, subject to the provisions of this Act, issue currency notes for one pound and for ten shillings and these notes shall be current in the United Kingdom in the same manner and to the same extent and as fully as sovereigns and half-sovereigns are current and shall be legal tender in the United Kingdom for the payment of any amount.

These currency notes were made convertible into gold coin on demand but, owing to the fact that gold had ceased to circulate, this particular clause did not become operative.

As regards the notes of the Bank of England, the Bank was allowed to issue notes in excess of the limit fixed by law, but this was only a temporary and emergency expedient and did not really affect the restriction imposed by the Act of 1844. The notes of the Bank were still convertible into gold, though during the war, and for some little time afterwards, the right of conversion was very little exercised.

From 1914 to 1925, owing to the restrictions on the export of gold and the difficulties put in the way of converting bank notes into gold coin, this country was practically off the Gold Standard, but in 1925 it was decided to return to the Gold Standard in the full sense of the term, and the same became law by the Gold Standard Act of that year. The main clauses which affected the Bank of England were as follows:

(1) The bank was released from its obligation under the Act of 1833 to redeem its notes in gold coin.

(2) Similarly, currency notes were also to be no longer convertible.

(3) The Bank was bound to sell gold in exchange for legal tender, that is, for bank notes or currency notes, at £3. 7s. 10½d. per ounce, but only in the form of bars of 400 ounces each.

A further change was made by the Currency and Bank Notes Act of 1928. This contained the very important provision that instead of having bank notes issued by the Bank, and currency notes issued by the Treasury, the two issues should be merged, and all the notes issued by the Bank of England. The total amount of the joint issue had to be covered partly by gold and partly by other forms of security, these now consisting of Government debt, other Government securities, other securities and silver coin. The amount not covered by gold, known as the "fiduciary issue", was fixed at £260,000,000: the total amount of note issue including those of £1 and 10s. thus being fixed at £260,000,000 plus the amount of the gold reserve. In August, 1931, with a view to preventing the amount of money in circulation being seriously diminished owing to the drain of gold which was then taking place, the Bank was authorized to issue for a period of three weeks a further £15,000,000 of fiduciary notes. This authorization was renewed from time to time, until on March 31, 1933, it was allowed to lapse and thus the fiduciary issue was as from that date reduced from £275,000,000 to the former figure of £260,000,000.

A further very important event in the Bank of England's history was the announcement on September 21, 1931, that, "Owing to the heavy drain of gold the Government had been obliged to suspend that section of the Gold Standard Act of 1925 by which the Bank of England was bound to sell gold in bars of not less than 400 ounces". This, in short, was an intimation that the country had been obliged to abandon the Gold Standard. The meaning of this step and some of its consequences will form the subject of a later chapter.[1]

NOTE

The following are the clauses of the "Currency and Bank Notes Act, 1928" referred to above:

Preamble

An Act to amend the law relating to the issue of bank notes by the Bank of England and by banks in Scotland and Northern Ireland, and to provide for the transfer to the Bank of England of the currency notes issue and of the assets appropriated for the redemption thereof, and to make certain provisions with respect to gold reserves and otherwise in connection with the matters aforesaid and to prevent the defacement of bank notes.

1. (1) (a) the Bank may issue bank notes for one pound and for ten shillings.

   (3) (a) notwithstanding anything in the proviso to section six of the Bank of England Act, 1833, bank notes for one

[1] Chapter XII.

pound or ten shillings shall be deemed a legal tender of payment by the Bank or any branch of the Bank, including payment of bank notes.

2. (1) Subject to the provisions of this Act the Bank shall issue bank notes up to the amount representing the gold coin and gold bullion for the time being in the issue department, and shall in addition issue bank notes to the amount of two hundred and sixty million pounds in excess of the amount first mentioned in this section, and the issue of notes which the Bank are by or under this Act required or authorized to make in excess of the said first mentioned amount is in this Act referred to as "the fiduciary note issue".

3. (1) In addition to the gold coin and bullion for the time being in the issue department, the Bank shall from time to time appropriate to and hold in the issue department securities of an amount in value sufficient to cover the fiduciary note issue for the time being.

8. (1) If the Bank at any time represent to the Treasury that it is expedient that the amount of the fiduciary note issue shall be increased to some specified amount above two hundred and sixty million pounds, the Treasury may authorize the Bank to issue bank notes to such an increased amount, not exceeding the amount specified as aforesaid, and for such period, not exceeding six months, as the Treasury think proper.

(2) Any authority so given may be renewed or varied from time to time on the like representation and in like manner:

Provided that, notwithstanding the foregoing provision, no such authority shall be renewed so as to remain in force (whether with or without variation) after the expiration of a period of two years from the date on which it was originally given, unless Parliament otherwise determines.

(3) Any minute of the Treasury authorizing an increase of the fiduciary note issue under this section shall be laid forthwith before both Houses of Parliament.

CHAPTER X

THE BANKS AT WORK

A very important feature of the English banking system is the connection which exists between the Bank of England and the ordinary banks of deposit, more generally known as the Joint Stock Banks. The Bank of England is often designated the "Bankers' Bank", partly because all other banks keep a large portion of their reserves with it, and partly because, apart from the fact that it does all the banking work for the Government, the banks are its principal customers. It may be useful, therefore, to examine our banking system first of all from the point of view of the banks in general, and then to link this up with the special conditions under which the operations of the Bank of England are carried on.

In banking, just as in most other economic matters, there is a tendency for people in general to look at things from their own personal point of view, and for them consequently to fail to appreciate the much wider considerations which concern the community as a whole.

From the point of view of the individual, the bank is merely an institution which keeps his money in greater safety than he can himself keep it, and lets him have it as he wants it; which receives his money on deposit, paying a small rate of interest for it; which occasionally allows him to overdraw his account; and which undertakes for him, if he is a business man, the discounting of bills and other similar services.

To him, then, the bank is one of the conveniences of life. His income, doubtless, will be received at more or less stated periods and in the form of money, of cheques or of dividend warrants. These then are paid into his account with the bank, and in this way he becomes the bank's creditor for such amounts. At the same time he is provided with a cheque-book, and draws cheques on his account as and when he needs to take out his money. These cheques may be drawn in favour of himself in order that he may be able to have cash for daily disbursements, or in favour of those to whom he owes money and to whom payment can more conveniently be made in this form. To the extent of these various withdrawals he is the bank's debtor. His pass-book contains the details of his deposits and withdrawals. It shows on opposite sides of the page what he pays in and what he takes out, the bank being his debtor for the former, and his creditor for the latter, the reverse of his own position as a customer of the bank. An account of this nature is generally known as a " Current Account", and is to be distinguished from another form of account which a customer may keep with the bank, viz. a "Deposit Account". The main difference between these two forms is that on current accounts no interest is paid and withdrawal can take place without notice, whereas on deposit accounts, which are in effect of the nature of loans to the bank, there is an agreed rate of interest and notice of withdrawal is required. The rate of interest on deposit accounts is generally $1\frac{1}{2}$ % to 2 % below the official bank rate, that is below the rate officially fixed by the Bank of England for its discounting of first-class bills.

A bank, on the other hand, may lend money to its customers and this is usually done by granting them a loan or an overdraft. This may be either a certain definite sum placed to the credit of the customer in the books of the bank, or it may be what is called "an overdraft facility", that is, overdrawing allowed up to a certain sum, and for this convenience the bank in either case charges a rate of interest usually about 1 % above bank rate with a minimum of 5 %. Except in cases where the customer's affairs are very intimately known to the bank and are considered to justify a departure from the ordinary practice, it is usual for the borrower to be required to furnish such security as in cases of default would allow the loan to be recovered without loss.

Just as in the case of the private individual, the business man or the joint stock company uses the bank as a convenient and safe place in which to keep all the incomings of the business, cheques being drawn for the various outgoings. With the private person an overdraft is as a rule a means of tiding over some special difficulty, such as may arise when income is received periodically in instalments and some particularly heavy payment has to be made in advance of the next quarter's salary, rents or dividends. With the business man the overdraft may almost be regarded as a regular part of his working arrangements. Wages have to be paid before the goods on which the labour is expended can be marketed and paid for, and the same is frequently the case with raw material and fuel, the cost of which is only recovered when the goods are sold. Hence there is a gap, and sometimes a very wide gap, between expenditure and revenue, and if this is not bridged by keeping a large balance at the bank, which can be drawn upon as needs arise, the customer will require overdraft facilities. Or it may happen that he has the opportunity of undertaking some large and important contract for which the costs to be incurred in advance would be very considerable and for which his cash resources would be inadequate. Under such circumstances he would probably go to the bank and ask for an advance of a fixed amount, undertaking to repay it at a given date by which time he might reasonably expect to have been himself paid by those who gave him the contract.

In the same way as with private overdrafts, business overdrafts may be with or without security. When overdraft facilities are required for the normal conduct of business, the circumstances of which are fully known to the bank, it is quite possible that security may not be demanded, though, if the bank were to perceive that orders were falling off and the receipts not coming in as regularly as before, it would probably make some sort of guarantee or security a condition of the continuance of the overdraft facilities. In the case, however, of an advance being required for some more particular transaction or project, security would probably be demanded, and this might possibly in some cases take the form of a long dated bill of exchange drawn by the manufacturer on a firm whose credit was deemed sufficiently good by the bank, this bill being discounted in the ordinary course of banking business. The granting of loans by way of overdrafts forms a very considerable part of the bank's business, the system being based on confidence in the customer's financial stability and on the adequacy of the security given. Outstanding overdrafts are being constantly reviewed by the bank, as any want of prudence in this matter would result in heavy loss.

It must always be borne in mind, however, that overdrafts are of the nature of short-period loans and consequently must not be confused with more permanent investments. English banks provide money not capital. The overdrafts they grant are as a rule for three or six months. They may be renewed when the period expires, but it is always understood that there is no obligation to extend the period beyond that for which the overdraft has been granted.

One of the greatest services which the bank renders to its business customers, and to the trading world in general, is the discounting of bills, to which reference has been made above. The length of credit given by the manufacturer or merchant to his customers depends partly on the usual practice in the particular line of business—for in some trades much longer credit is given than in others—and partly on the financial position of the individual customer. If this customer, however, is not personally known to him, or he has any uncertainty about his circumstances, he will doubtless refer to what is known as a "Commercial Status Inquiry Office" for a credit report on his business standing.

In this matter of the time allowed for the payment of accounts some difference is generally made between home and export orders. The main object of giving credit is to allow the customer time to receive the goods, and in some cases even to dispose of them, before payment for them is made, and it stands to reason that if the customer is in a distant part of the world there may be quite a considerable interval between the dispatch of the goods and their receipt by the customer who has ordered them.

For home orders, especially with regular customers, no formal undertaking to pay is as a rule demanded. Transactions of this kind are sometimes for cash, but more generally a month is allowed for payment. In foreign trade, on the other hand, it is not unusual to allow two months' or even three months' credit, and as it would not be convenient for the exporter to wait so long for his money, while at the same time he wants to have something in the way of a definite undertaking to pay, he draws a bill on the customer, which is in effect an order to him to pay the amount due at a certain future date. When such bills have been accepted by the customer they then become negotiable instruments, and so if the exporter finds it inconvenient to wait for his money till a bill falls due, he can discount it with the bank and in this way receive immediate cash for his account, the bank deducting interest for the unexpired period of the bill at the current discount rate.

Bills of exchange play a very important part in all matters of international trade and finance, but this aspect of the subject will be more fully dealt with in a later chapter.[1]

Hitherto the subject of banking has been dealt with from the point of view of the customer: it remains to look at it from the point of view of the banks themselves and of the way they serve to promote the convenience and well-being of the community as a whole. From the customers' point of view the

[1] See Chapter XIII.

bank has come to be regarded as one of the essentials of everyday life, without which the complicated transactions of the modern business world would be practically impossible. From the point of view of the community the bank is part of a financial system on which the whole of the industry and trade of the country depends. Without adequate finance the economic life of the community could not go on, and as finance is in the hands of the banks, their control of it brings with it a heavy responsibility: the due recognition of which by the great banks of the country forms the corner-stone of our banking system. This is, however, not the only responsibility which rests upon the banks, for as joint stock companies they have a responsibility to their shareholders, and as banks of deposit they have a responsibility to their depositors. The shareholders have provided the capital and they expect the directors of the particular bank to earn dividends for them. But this must always be subsidiary to the interests of the depositors, for if at any time there were reason to suppose that the depositors were not fully and adequately protected, the credit of the bank would suffer to such an extent that even its continued existence might be seriously threatened. It is in this respect that the English banking system differs in the main from that which exists in foreign countries generally. The interests of the depositors would be jeopardized if the banks were to take an active part in industry or trade, or were to invest their funds in business undertakings. Owing to their adherence to this policy of assisting trade and industry without participating in the risks incidental to them, English banks have been accused of being too conservative and too much behind the times, but the inherent strength of the English system and the value of that strength to the whole community have been well demonstrated throughout the times of financial strain which have been experienced since 1914.

The way in which the banks discharge their duty both to their customers and to the community may best be illustrated

by taking a practical example. By the courtesy of the directors
of Barclays Bank, one of the largest and most important of our
banking institutions, the author is allowed to quote some
figures from a recent Balance Sheet showing the financial
position of the bank as at December 31, 1931.

In this connection the two questions which it is now sought
to answer are briefly:

(1) What funds has a bank at its disposal with which it
can carry on its business? Or, in other words, what
are its resources?

and (2) How does it dispose of such funds with a view to
discharging its threefold responsibility—administer-
ing the property of its shareholders, safeguarding the
interests of its depositors, and assisting the trade of
the country?

(1) THE BANK'S RESOURCES

These may be divided into two classes: those which are
provided by the shareholders, and those which are provided
by the depositors. The former would include the issued share
capital, the reserve fund and the balance carried into the
Balance Sheet from the Profit and Loss Account. The latter
would include balances on current accounts, deposit accounts,
and balances in account with subsidiary banks.

As already pointed out in the chapter dealing with the
Balance Sheet, the Reserve Fund is the amount of undis-
tributed profits from previous years, and the balance from
the Profit and Loss Account represents the profits of the year
under review, together with the balance of the Profit and Loss
Account carried forward from the previous year. These two
amounts, therefore, are properly classed with the issued
capital as forming the total of the funds provided by the
shareholders.

The essential difference between the shareholders' money
and the depositors' money is that the latter is subject to with-

drawal and the former is not. Hence, when we look at the
other side of the Balance Sheet to see how the bank uses the
resources at its disposal, one of the most important things to
notice is the provision which the bank has made for meeting
possible withdrawals from the current and deposit accounts.

(2) HOW THE BANK EMPLOYS THE FUNDS AT ITS DISPOSAL

Omitting the item of Buildings, etc., £6,750,000, as being
definitely of the nature of "fixed assets", and that of
Customers' Acceptances, which appears also on the other
side of the Balance Sheet, it is possible to arrange the other
assets in the following descending order of liquidity:

		£
1.	Cash in hand and with the Bank of England and other Cash Balances	56,950,000
2.	Money at Call and Short Notice	21,750,000
3.	Bills Discounted	40,800,000
4.	Investments	63,250,000
5.	Advances to Customers	172,200,000

Together amounting to £354,950,000

These need to be examined in detail, as it is on the liquidity
of its assets that the ability of the bank to meet all emergencies
depends.

(1) *Cash in hand and with the Bank of England*

This item must be taken to include balances kept with
other British banks and cheques in course of collection, as
they also are practically equivalent to cash in hand. This is
the money which the bank has immediately available to meet
the withdrawals which may daily take place at its head office
and at the various branches. It is not sufficient merely to
keep in this form enough cash to meet what may be called the
ordinary business requirements, but there must be some
margin provided against exceptional withdrawals. The proportion of the deposits which according to sound practice the

SPECIMEN BANK BALANCE SHEET[1]

Dr. Liabilities	£	s.	d.	Assets	£	s.	d. Cr.
Current, Deposit and other Accounts, including Balances in account with Subsidiary Banks	333,250,000	0	0	Cash in hand and with Bank of England and other Cash Balances (=17%)	56,950,000	0	0
Issued Capital	15,850,000	0	0	Money at Call and Short Notice (=6½%)	21,750,000	0	0
Reserve Fund	10,250,000	0	0	Bills Discounted (=12%)	40,800,000	0	0
Balance from Profit and Loss	2,350,000	0	0	Advances to Customers	172,200,000	0	0
Acceptances, etc., for Customers	10,800,000	0	0	Investments (=19%) (=51½%)	63,250,000	0	0
					354,950,000	0	0
				Buildings, etc.	6,750,000	0	0
				Liability of Customers for Acceptances	10,800,000	0	0
	£372,500,000	0	0		£372,500,000	0	0

[1] The wording of the Balance Sheet has been much abridged with a view to bringing out more clearly the essential features. For the same reason the figures are given in round numbers. The arrangement of the items and the deductions from the figures have been made by the author.

bank will arrange to have actually in hand to meet withdrawals will differ naturally very much from district to district. For example, in a manufacturing district there would be a large amount taken out at the end of each week for the payment of wages, whereas in a purely residential neighbourhood the withdrawals would for the most part only be for household and other current expenses. The surplus of cash in any branch over and above what is required to meet current needs is sent by the Branch to its Head Office and if not needed there is deposited with the Bank of England.

(2) *Money at Call and Short Notice*

Next in liquidity to the cash in hand comes money at call and short notice, that is, money lent from day to day at a low rate of interest which can be called in at very short notice should the bank need this portion of its resources to meet exceptional withdrawals or for any other purpose. The rate of interest obtained for these short loans varies with two things:

(1) The Bank Rate.

(2) The quantity of money available in the money market to meet the current demands.

At a time when the bank rate is 5 %, the day-to-day loans might bring anything between $2\frac{1}{2}$ % and 4 % and loans at short notice about $3\frac{1}{2}$ % or 4 %, but if the bank rate were as low as 2 %, the rate for day-to-day loans might not be more than $\frac{1}{2}$ % to $\frac{3}{4}$ % and money at short notice very slightly if anything higher.

(3) *Bills Discounted*

This method of employing the funds of the bank presupposes that the money is not likely to be needed immediately or at very short notice, and that consequently it may be used for this form of short investment. Discounting bills is really buying Bills of Exchange, that is, buying the right to receive money at a future date, and paying for these bills in cash a sum equal to their face value less interest on the sum paid for the period which must elapse before they fall due and the bank can collect the full amount written on them. In this way it is using part of its deposits to bring in an income by lending money at a higher rate than could be obtained if it were lent at call or short notice. Again the factors determining the rate of interest that can be charged are the bank rate and the relation there is between the demand for and the supply of money for discounting purposes existing in the money market at the time. Supposing, for example, that 5 % was the minimum rate at which the Bank of England would discount what are known as "bank bills", we should expect the discount rate of the other banks to be rather less than this, say between 4 % and 5 %. For "trade bills" the rate would be somewhat higher than for bank bills, according to the length of time which has to elapse before the bill falls due and the character of the risk.

(4) *Investments*

The liquidity of investments depends very much on their character. Those in the form of stocks and shares can be sold either for cash, as is the case with Government securities, or for payment at the next Stock Exchange settlement. They may be sold at a profit or at a loss according to the difference between the market prices ruling at the times of purchase and sale respectively. In this they differ from advances which have to be repaid in full.

(5) *Advances*

Advances usually take the form of a Loan, which is really an entry in the books of the bank crediting the customer with a sum over and above the amount which he has deposited. In the bank's accounts the Loan would appear both as a debit and as a credit, for on the one side the deposits would be increased, and so would also the amount of advances on the other. Let us follow this statement out by taking a practical example: A certain customer has been granted a Loan of say £10,000, and his current account has been credited with it just the same as if he had actually paid that amount into the bank. Since this amount is now standing to his credit he is enabled to draw cheques against it, and the mere fact that he was in want of this Loan suggests that in all probability he would before long draw the whole of this amount out. In the meantime the situation is as follows: £10,000 has appeared among the deposits, and £10,000 also among the advances, and so far the bank's position remains unchanged, for the same sum has appeared on both sides of the bank's accounts.

Taking the original amount of the deposits as X, the amount of cash as Y, and the amount of advances as Z, the effect of giving the customer the Loan may be shown as follows:

FIGURE A

Dr.   Cr.

Deposits	$X + £10,000$	Cash	Y
		Advances	$Z + £10,000$

But after the customer has drawn out in cash the whole of the £10,000 the effect will be

(1) That the deposits are now reduced by £10,000, because the customer has no longer this amount to draw upon.

(2) That advances will still show an increase of £10,000, because the customer still owes this amount to the bank.

(3) That cash has gone out to the extent of £10,000, thus reducing the item Cash in hand by this amount.

This may also be shown diagrammatically in the same way:

FIGURE B

Dr.			Cr.
Deposits	X	Cash	$Y - £10,000$
		Advances	$Z + £10,000$

In neither case has the balance of the account been affected in any way, but the bank's position is weaker, for owing to its cash being reduced, its power to meet withdrawals is diminished. Hence prudence would set a limit to the giving of Loans, for even if we may assume that the bank holds securities for all its Loans, and consequently its resources have not suffered in any way, yet its liquidity, that is its immediate cash position, is not so good as it was.

We may, however, follow up the transaction a little further and see what happens to the £10,000 that was drawn out in cash. The persons who received the money, for let us suppose that the customer who got the advance wanted it to pay his wages bill and so would have drawn the money out in this form, would proceed to spend it in various ways such as on food, clothing, rent, etc. The tradesman or the landlord would periodically deposit the amount so received with his own bank—it might be the same bank or it might be another—and hence it would not be long before the cash of some bank or other would be increased. Let us assume the case of a small town with one large factory and only one bank which, shall we say, is a branch of one of the "Big Five". In this case the tradesmen and the landlords would probably all be local people and therefore the money, or the greater part of it, would come back to the same bank as had granted the Loan and had paid out the amount in cash; under such circumstances the liquidity of the bank would be at once restored to its former position, for the customer who got the advance would still owe it to the bank, while the balance at the bank of the other customers had been increased with the result that the cash position had also been improved. The situation thus created would now be as follows:

FIGURE C

Dr.   *Cr.*

Deposits $X + £10,000$ Cash Y

                                         Advances $Z + £10,000$

The only difference from the situation shown in Figure A being that what was there credited to the customer who got the Loan is now credited to the other customers who received it in payment for goods, etc., and paid it into their respective accounts.

If we were to increase the size of the area, the number of manufacturing concerns and the number of banks carrying on business within it, the situation would not be very different. The bank doing the largest business would make the largest number of advances and have also the largest number of individual customers, whose deposits would be swollen by the money spent in their shops.

It is more than probable that advances by way of Loans made to its customers by any one of the banks in the town would result in the money withdrawn on the strength of these advances being spent in shops the proprietors of which kept their accounts with certain of the other banks doing business there. These banks in their turn out of the cash deposited would be in a position to make further advances to their own customers, who would use the money they obtained to make payments of various kinds. The money would thus pass on to other persons, some of whom at any rate would be customers of the bank first mentioned.

With the money circulating in this way the general result would be a continual tendency towards a return to the *status quo*, and it would be found that in the long run matters would so have adjusted themselves that, with a fair amount of exactitude, the financial position of the respective banks would be in accordance with the relative amounts of business they were doing.

In this way it will be seen that what is advanced by one bank may become, and quite frequently does become, the deposits of another, and as these deposits in their turn give rise to other advances there will be a further result of deposits being made somewhere else, and hence there is a kind of endless chain—deposits giving rise to advances, advances leading to fresh deposits, these deposits being again advanced and so on *ad infinitum*.

The ultimate effect of the transaction would have been in no way different if, in the above example, the customer who obtained the loan, instead of drawing out the sum advanced to him in cash and distributing it in that form amongst his workpeople, had used it for some other purposes, such as the purchase of raw material, tools, or fuel. In this case he would doubtless have drawn cheques for the various amounts, and the recipients of them would in due course have paid them into the banks with which they themselves kept an account. The deposits of these banks would then be increased by the several amounts paid in precisely in the same way as if the new deposits had been as first suggested in the form of currency.

Cheques play so important a part in business life that it is worth while considering in more detail the way they operate. In the first place it should be noticed that cheques are not money, but they take the place of money. They are not legal tender and yet they are to a large extent accepted without hesitation and without inquiry. The cheque is accepted in payment of sums due on the supposition

(1) That the drawer has an account with the bank in question.

(2) That he has sufficient funds in that account to meet the cheque when presented.

If either of these should not prove to be the case payment would be refused and the cheque handed back marked " R.D. ", that is to say, " Refer to drawer ". The mere fact that there must be confidence in the person who draws the cheque or it would not be accepted makes it to be a credit instrument and not money in the strict sense of the term. Another difference is that whereas money in the form of currency notes or coin can be used in making payments over and over again, a cheque can only be used for a single transaction. When it has once been cashed or paid into a banking account its work is done, and the bank returns it to the customer for him to keep as an acknowledgment on the part of the payee, that is, the person in whose favour the cheque has been drawn, that the debt has been paid.

It will thus be seen that by the use of cheques there is an immense saving of currency. Business payments to the extent of thousands of millions of pounds are made in the course of a year without currency at all, merely by making entries in the books of the different banks that so much has been deposited or so much withdrawn. This becomes possible only through the fact that most people have banking accounts and that, except for comparatively small sums, most people pay what they owe by means of cheques.

A cheque is merely an order on the bank with which the drawer keeps an account to pay to a third person the specified sum. In this respect it resembles a Bill of Exchange but it differs from a Bill of Exchange in one essential particular. A bill is an order to the person on whom it is drawn, not necessarily a bank, to pay the sum named on it *at some future date*, a cheque is always drawn on a bank and is payable *at sight*.

As already said, the majority of cheques drawn are not cashed by the payee but are paid by him into his account with some bank. It is for that bank then to obtain payment from the bank on which the cheque was drawn. Between these banks, however, there are likely, even in the course of a single day, to be many transactions in both directions, Bank *A* holding cheques drawn on Bank *B*, and Bank *B* some drawn on Bank *A*. All that is necessary, therefore, is to compare the respective amounts and for a cheque to be given for the difference.

THE BANKERS' CLEARING HOUSE

From this much simplified illustration we must pass to the more complicated conditions of banking as a whole. The fact that the number of banking houses is very large, though a very large proportion of the banking business is in the hands of the "Big Five", and that each of them is holding every day cheques drawn on most if not all of the others, tends to make the task of "clearing", as it is called, one of very considerable magnitude and importance. The work is done at the Bankers' Clearing House in Lombard Street. The leading London banks are members of the Clearing House; other banks, including Country banks, are represented there by one of the Clearing House Banks. To the Clearing House comes each day someone from each of these banks bringing with him the numerous cheques drawn on other banks which have been paid in by its customers. The cheques are then sorted out and an account is drawn up for each bank, showing what it has to pay and what it has to receive. The balance, on whichever side it happens to be, whether in favour of the bank or against it, is then liquidated by means of a cheque drawn on the Bank of England, with which institution as already mentioned each of the banks must of necessity keep an account. In this way the greater part of the home trade of the country is carried on by means of orders to pay which in the majority of cases are made to cancel out one another.

The weekly return of the Bankers' Clearing House gives the total of the cheques cleared during the previous week. This may vary enormously according to the general condition

of trade, but in any case it amounts to an almost fabulous sum.
Thus for the first week of 1931 the total amounted to about
£930 millions, while that for the corresponding week of 1932
was some £646 millions.

CONCLUSION

It has thus been seen that in many different ways the
English Joint Stock Banks render a service to the business
community that is absolutely indispensable. They receive
deposits from the public and thus accumulate a store of
wealth which can be drawn on not only for purposes of consumption but also for purposes of production, for the many
small balances, which could not singly be put to any productive
use, when massed together form an enormous fund for assisting the business life of the community by the making of advances and the discounting of Bills of Exchange. In addition,
through the cheque system they provide a simple and yet
most effective machinery by which money can be transferred
and debts paid without making any demands upon the currency resources of the country.

A good deal has been said about the necessity of the banks
maintaining a strong liquid position, that is to say one in
which they are always prepared to meet any probable demands
for the withdrawal of deposits. If we now turn once more
to the Balance Sheet given on p. 143 the significance of the
percentages inserted after each of the items on the "Assets"
side will become apparent.

Cash in hand represents approximately 17 % of the De-
posits, Money at Short Notice 6½ %, Bills Discounted 12 %,
Investments 19 % and Advances to Customers 51½ %.
Further, since it is very probable that some at any rate of the
Bills Discounted are nearing maturity, and all of them in case
of real need could be turned into cash by re-discounting them,
it may be said that according to the figures of this Balance
Sheet some 35½ % of the deposits are in a form either im-

mediately available in cash or convertible into cash with comparatively little delay. It is possible also that some portion of the Investments could be, if necessary, sold, and some portion of the Advances could be readily called in or terminated, the borrowers being required to return the loans in question or being informed that expiring loans cannot be renewed. This being the case, it is evident that though money which has taken the form either of Investments or of Advances cannot be regarded as being actually liquid, yet a portion of the 19 % in the one case and of the 51½ % in the other, could be made so if sufficient time were allowed.

The question then arises, what is the proportion of Cash in hand to the Deposits which may be regarded as a reasonable margin of safety? The knowledge and experience gained by many years of banking in bad times as well as in good can alone supply a satisfactory answer. This proportion is sometimes stated to be as low as 10 % or 12 %, but a more conservative figure, perhaps, would be in the neighbourhood of 15 %, and hence the 17 % shown on this Balance Sheet is seen to be well above this line.

If, as might conceivably happen, there should be some general nervousness, some want of public confidence, which would lead to the sudden withdrawal of deposits on a large scale, the cash in hand would be the first line of defence. There are, however, behind it, as has been shown above, reserve forces of varying strength which can be called up in support, though these would require a shorter or longer time to mobilize. Without then being able to lay down any hard and fast line as to where the margin of safety actually lies and to which all banks should more or less closely conform, it may yet be taken for granted that an adequate margin will always be preserved by all British banks of repute, and that the measures taken by them to safeguard the liquidity of their position will at all times be of such a nature as to place their stability and solvency beyond all question or possibility of doubt.

CHAPTER XI

THE BANK OF ENGLAND

Having considered the working of the English banking system from the point of view of the Joint Stock Banks, we must now examine a little more closely the operations of the Bank of England and the part it plays in the financial life of the community.

The story of the founding of the Bank of England given in Chapter IX should have made it quite clear that it is not in any sense a Government institution, for it was started by private enterprise and with private capital, and is in fact a Joint Stock Company. Like any other company the direction of its affairs is in the hands of a Board of Directors, officially known as the "Court" of the Bank, at the head of which are the "Governor" and the "Deputy Governor". But unlike any other company the Directors are elected not by the shareholders but by the Court of Directors itself.

Another point worthy of note is that the Directors of the Bank of England cannot be themselves bankers: they may be engaged in other branches of finance or they may be business men of high standing and repute.

The conduct of the Bank's affairs is quite independent of Government control, but at the same time there is a very close association between the Bank and the Treasury, the Bank keeping that Department of State closely in touch with the financial position in general, and the Treasury consulting the Bank as to the probable effect of any financial change contemplated. Hence there is very little doubt that the Treasury is able to bring a certain amount of pressure to bear on the policy of the Bank, and the Bank on the other hand is in a position to exercise some influence over the financial policy of the Government.

There is also a purely business relationship between the Treasury and the Bank, for the latter acts as the Government's financial agent. It keeps the Government banking account, it makes advances when called upon to do so, it places on the market all the Government loans, and it arranges for the sale of short-term Treasury Bills whenever there is need of anticipating revenue by raising money in this way. Further, in its hands is the regulating of the currency supply, for though the conditions of issue are prescribed by Act of Parliament, the amount of the issue, so far as that part of it which is covered by gold is concerned, can be varied from time to time by the action of the Bank. How this is done will be explained later on.

Mention has already been made of the division of the Bank into two departments, the Issue Department and the Banking Department; an arrangement which was introduced by the Bank Charter Act of 1844. In the weekly return the position of each of these departments is shown separately, as will be seen by the following example, which is the return for the week ending February 17, 1932.

BANK OF ENGLAND RETURN

February 17, 1932

Issue Department

Dr.			Cr.
Notes issued:		Government debt ...	£11,015,100
In circulation ...	£344,882,554	Other Government se-	
In Banking Depart-		curities	251,294,351
ment	50,883,927	Other securities ...	8,842,388
		Silver coin	3,848,161
		Amount of fiduciary issue	£275,000,000
		Gold coin and bullion	120,766,481
	£395,766,481		£395,766,481

Banking Department

Dr.					Cr.
Capital	£14,553,000	Government securities	£33,495,906
Rest	3,640,793	Other securities:	
Public deposits[1] ...	15,358,981	Discounts and advances	11,944,547
Other deposits:		Securities	39,124,051
Bankers	70,455,852	Notes	50,883,927
Other accounts ...	31,988,874	Gold and silver coin...	551,106
Seven-day and other bills	2,037		
	£135,999,537		£135,999,537

[1] Including Exchequer, Savings Banks, Commissioners of National Debt and Dividend accounts.

THE ISSUE DEPARTMENT

On the debit side of the Issue Department's account we have "Notes issued", and these are given under two headings, viz. notes "in circulation" and notes "in Banking Department", which added together make up the total amount of the note issue, viz. £395,766,481. It will be noticed that the notes given as "in Banking Department" also appear on the credit side of that department's account as forming a part of the security which the Bank holds against its deposits and other liabilities. So long as these notes remain in the Banking Department, they may be regarded, from the point of view of currency, as virtually withdrawn from circulation.

On the credit side of the Issue Department's account we find set out the items composing what is called the "cover" for the note issue. The last of these items, "Gold coin and bullion", is what is generally spoken of as the "Gold Reserve", and above that is the total amount of the "Fiduciary Issue", that is of notes covered otherwise than by gold. It has already been pointed out that by the Act of 1928 the amount of the fiduciary issue was fixed at 260 millions, and that in August, 1931, at the time of the crisis, this was increased by another 15 millions making 275 millions in all.

Above the line we have the "cover" of the fiduciary issue, and this is given under four headings: "Government debt", "Other Government securities", "Other securities" and "Silver coin".

By a simple calculation it will now become evident that on February 17, 1932, the Bank of England notes in issue were covered to the extent of about 30 % by gold, and about 70 % by securities—mostly Government stock—and silver coin. Or taking into consideration the fact that nearly 51 millions of the notes were at this date in the Banking Department, and so for the time being not in circulation, the percentage of gold to the notes actually circulating works out approximately at 35 %.

THE BANKING DEPARTMENT

Turning to the account of the Banking Department we have here a statement somewhat similar to that contained in the specimen Bank Balance Sheet given on p. 143. On the debit side we have the resources of the Bank, which we may divide up as before into what is provided by the shareholders and what is provided by the depositors. The shareholders' contribution is again divided up into "Capital" and "Rest", the latter being the term used to denote the "Reserve Fund" built up out of previous profits, and which in the case of one of the other banks would appear under that name. In the case of the Bank of England, the term "Reserve" is applied to the "Notes" and "Gold and silver coin", the last two items on the credit side. These would in the case of one of the other banks be entered as "Cash in hand". This use of the term "Reserve" is quite distinct from the "Gold Reserve", which has already been referred to in connection with the Issue Department. There is, however, one important difference between the "Rest" and what is normally called "Reserves". Reserves as they appear in the annual balance sheet of a company are a fixed amount definitely set aside from profits at an annual meeting, but the "Rest" may fluctuate from week to week, for it consists not merely of a sum set aside from past profits but also of some of the current profits, and thus prior to the distribution of a dividend the "Rest" is generally considerably enlarged. After the distribution it is proportionally reduced, but it is a more or less fixed practice not to allow the amount of the "Rest" to fall below the 3 million mark.

The deposits are given under three headings: "Public deposits", that is the amount standing to the credit of the Government; "Bankers' deposits", the sum total of the balances kept at the Bank of England by all the other banks; and "other accounts", being the deposits of the Bank's customers other than the Government and the banks. The last two of these items will probably include quite a number of book credits, and as such credits will have been given against securities, a corresponding amount should be looked for on the credit side as part of the sum given under that heading.

Under "Public deposits", as already mentioned, we have the balance of the Government account with the Bank. This is naturally a very inconstant item, for it is affected on the one hand by revenue received, which when collected is placed to the credit of the Government's account, and on the other by Government expenditure and by the payment of dividends on consols and other Government stocks, for which purposes money is withdrawn from that account. During the first three months of the year when the income tax is being paid the amount may be considerably increased and similarly, when expenditure has the upper hand, as it has during the months April to December, it may be considerably diminished. For example, "Public deposits" were on December 2, 1931, £8,593,824 and on February 17, 1932, when quite a considerable portion of the income tax had been collected, it was £15,358,981.

THE "PROPORTION"

Like any other bank, the Bank of England must keep a sufficient proportion of its deposits in such a form that it can instantly meet any possible demands for withdrawals which may be made upon it, and inasmuch as the Bank of England is the guardian of the cash balances of all other banks, with it lies in the last resort the responsibility for maintaining the solvency of the credit system of the country as a whole. Cash in hand or immediately available to the extent of 15 % of its deposits may be regarded as ample, or more than ample, for one of the big joint stock banks, but this would not be sufficient for the Bank of England. Comparing the weekly returns of the Bank extending over a period of some months, we should find that the "Proportion", as it is called, is maintained for the most part at round about 40 %. The "Proportion" is arrived at by taking the total of the deposits, which in the return for February 17, 1932, come to about 118 millions, and comparing this sum with the notes and coin forming the cash reserve, together amounting to about 51½ millions. This gives us a percentage of cash to deposits of just under 44 %.

It should, however, be noticed that at different times of the year and under different circumstances the "Proportion" may show very marked fluctuations. For example, the Bank Return of September 23, 1931 (the one following the abandonment of the Gold Standard on September 20), showed a "Proportion" of Reserve to Deposits of 41¼ %. The preceding week it had been 48 %, and in the corresponding week of 1930, no less than 55 %. This would suggest that at a time when the Bank was exposed to withdrawals of gold on foreign account it was apt to maintain a higher "Proportion" than when this danger was removed.

Again, if we compare January, 1932, with the same month in 1931, we shall find an equally marked difference, not only

between those two months but also between the beginning
of January and other times of the year. On January 7, 1932,
the "Proportion" was only $24\frac{5}{8}$ % and the previous week it
was still lower at $18\frac{7}{16}$, whereas the figure for the corresponding
week of 1931 was $37\frac{5}{16}$.

Looking at the Bank's other assets, we find that these are
classed as "Government securities", "Discounts and advances", and "Securities". Exact comparison between these
and the corresponding items on the credit side of the specimen Balance Sheet given on p. 143 is not easy to draw.
Government securities may be taken as "investments", and
"discounts" are doubtless the same in both cases, but it is
not clearly shown whether Government securities are the
only investments, or to what extent advances to customers are
referred to under the heading "Securities". These, however,
are mainly questions of terminology and arrangement.
Putting them on one side, it will be seen that one of the main
differences between the banking method of the Bank of
England and that of other banks is that a very much larger
part of the Bank's resources takes the form of Cash in hand
and Investments, and a correspondingly smaller part that of
Advances against securities.

THE BANK AND MONEY SUPPLY

Arising out of the fact that the Bank of England holds the
gold reserve of the country, it is in the position of being able,
through its regulation of that reserve, to exercise a controlling
influence over the whole money supply of the country. We
are here using the term money in the wider sense in which it
is used in the world of business, that is to say, we are regarding money as being in effect all that is available for the purpose
of making purchases or of settling debts. This may be done
by cash or by some credit instrument such as a cheque, and
for this purpose both forms may be regarded as money, and
as people in general put the money they receive into a bank

and draw it out when they want it by means of cheques, it may well be said that the person who owns money has the right to draw cheques. Moreover, since the majority of a bank's customers rarely if ever leave their account entirely without funds, bankers are in a position to lend these balances to others of their customers by giving them loans and over-drafts, that is, the right to draw cheques on what is really an artificially created deposit in their books. Whether in the form of cash or of credit, the amount of money available at any given time depends in the last resort on the gold reserve of the Bank of England.

Beginning with money in the form of cash, and omitting for the purpose of this argument those forms of it which are represented by silver or copper coins, as these are only sub-sidiary currency and are legal tender only for a limited amount, we will take the term cash as being equivalent to note issue. If we look at the Bank Return from week to week, we shall notice that the total amount of the note issue is continually changing, but one part of it, the fiduciary issue, does not change in amount, for, as said above, under the Currency and Bank Notes Act of 1928 the amount is legally fixed at 260 millions.[1] On the application of the Bank of England, how-ever, the Treasury is empowered to authorize an increase in the fiduciary issue, and it was in consequence of such applica-tion that on August 2, 1931, when the Bank was anxious that the drain of gold should not unduly diminish the quantity of notes in circulation, the Treasury authorized that increase of 15 millions, for a period of three weeks, which raised the total of the authorized fiduciary issue to 275 millions. The authorization is only for a stated period, and hence, to main-tain the issue at this higher figure, it has to be continually renewed.[2] Since, then, the total note issue amounts to the fiduciary issue plus the gold reserve, and the former is a fixed

[1] See Note which follows Chapter IX, p. 133.
[2] On March 31, 1933, the fiduciary issue again became £260,000,000.

amount, any fluctuations must be due to changes in the amount of the gold reserve. This is clearly seen from the four following examples:

(1) On July 9, 1931, when the fiduciary issue was fixed at 260 millions and the gold reserve was 166 millions, the total note issue amounted to 426 millions, the percentage of gold to notes being about 39 %.

(2) A fortnight later, when the fiduciary issue was still 260 millions, the gold reserve was down to 150 millions, and the total note issue stood at 410 millions. Percentage about 36%.

(3) On September 23, 1931, after the fiduciary issue had been increased to 275 millions, the gold reserve was a little over 133 millions, and the note issue accordingly was 408 millions odd. Percentage about 32%.

(4) On February 17, 1932, with the fiduciary issue still 275 millions and the gold reserve down to 120 millions, the note issue was reduced to 395 millions. Percentage about 30%.

Thus we are able to say that the volume of currency issued depends on the gold reserve, as also do changes in the percentages of gold to the total note issue, for as the amount of the fiduciary part of it, apart from temporarily authorized increases or decreases, can only be altered by Act of Parliament, it may be regarded, for the time being at least, as a constant factor. This is not the case with many foreign currencies, for with them a minimum percentage of gold to notes is the fixed quantity—generally about 40%—and the amount of the fiduciary issue varies in accordance with the changes in the amount of the gold reserve.

Turning to the other element of money in the wider sense of purchasing medium, namely credit, it can also be said that the credit of the country depends on the gold reserve at the Bank of England. We have already seen that credit is created by the banks, as also by the Bank of England, through the simple process of making advances to their customers. In making these advances the banks are not restricted in any way. They exercise their judgment as to the extent to which it may be considered prudent to create credits of this kind, bearing in mind that these credits are liable to result in cash withdrawals, and that "Cash in hand and with the Bank of England" must therefore be sufficient to meet all demands that are likely to be made upon them.

At the same time, it is usual to state that the volume of the credit given by the banks is an edifice erected on the foundation of the Bank of England's gold reserve. To illustrate this, let us refer again to the specimen Balance Sheet given on p. 143. This, as already noticed, shows "Cash in hand and with the Bank of England and other cash balances" amounting to 57 millions as against deposits of various kinds of 334 millions, or approximately 17 %. Of these 57 millions, a portion, the exact amount of which is not given in the balance sheet, is cash at the Bank of England. For the sake of argument, let us assume that this amounts to some 10 millions, which will now form part of the "Banker's deposits" shown in the Bank of England return. As already explained, the Bank of England holds a cash reserve against these deposits of a varying amount, but for our purpose let us take this as being 40 %. Then, of the 10 millions deposited by this bank, 40 %, or 4 millions, is kept in reserve by the Bank of England against it. But the reserve is in notes, and these are only partially covered by gold, that is, to the extent of 30 %, which was the figure shown in the return of February 17, 1932. Taking then 30 % of the 4 millions, which works out at somewhat less than $1\frac{1}{4}$ millions, we find that in the credit edifice built up by the said deposits of 334 millions are depending on a cash in hand of 57 millions, and that this in turn rests on a gold basis of less than $1\frac{1}{4}$ millions, a proportion of gold to deposits of only $\frac{2}{5}$ of 1 %.

THE GOLD BASIS

The stability of the gold basis, on which our credit system rests, may be said therefore to be dependent upon the relation existing at any time between the gold reserve and the total note issue. It has already been pointed out that on July 9, 1931, the note issue was 426 millions and the gold reserve 166 millions, a percentage not of 30% but of 39%. It is evident, therefore, that now we are off the gold standard our credit edifice is being supported by a smaller foundation of gold than it was before. Going off the gold standard meant that bank notes were no longer convertible into gold on demand, hence the gold reserve is no longer threatened by withdrawals on this account, and consequently a smaller amount of gold is able to discharge its function of supporting the credit which forms part of the country's money supply.

It has often been objected that our gold basis is not sufficiently broad to support the very large credit edifice erected upon it. Before we abandoned the gold standard it was very frequently urged that the Bank was not maintaining a gold reserve equal to the very heavy amount of credit work it was called upon to perform. Since September, 1931, however, this question has somewhat dropped into the background, but it is very probable that if and when we return to a gold standard this question will again come up for serious consideration.

It is generally admitted that the shortage in the available world supply of gold has been one of the main causes of the recent low level of prices and the consequent trade depression so generally prevailing. Hence, many suggestions have been made for remedying this serious condition of affairs. Some economists have advocated a more economic use of gold, that is, making a smaller amount of gold than has been the case hitherto perform an equal amount of work in the supporting of credit, or in other words altering the proportion between the fiduciary issue and the gold reserve in favour of the former. Others, looking at the problem more particularly as it affects this country, have advocated the doing away of the separation between the Issue and Banking Departments of the Bank of England and utilizing their joint reserves of gold and notes as one united cash reserve. Discussion of questions such as these, however, would lead us beyond the limits of the present book; it must suffice, therefore, to make this brief reference to them.

THE GENERAL LEVEL OF PRICES

It has already been pointed out that the purchasing power of the community consists partly of currency and partly of credit, and that both of these are based on the Bank of England's gold reserve. It is a widely accepted principle that the general price level at any time bears a definite relation to the total amount of purchasing power available; that an increase in purchasing power normally results in a higher price level and a decrease in a lower one. This being so, the conclusion is inevitable that the general price level is dependent on gold reserve, and this is another of the considerations which brings the policy of the Bank of England into such a close relationship with the general course of trade and industry.

We must not, however, suppose either that the quantity of gold in the Bank of England is the only factor causing a general rise or fall in prices, or that when there is such a rise or fall it is reflected equally in the prices of all commodities. The general price level is an average obtained from the prices of a certain number of articles of general consumption, raw materials as well as food. This average when ascertained is expressed as a percentage of the average which obtained at some particular date and which is taken as the standard of reference. This percentage is usually spoken of as an "Index Number". *The Times* publishes an Index Number at the beginning of each month based on 22 articles of food and 38 materials which are used industrially. The average price for these during the year 1913 is taken as the standard and is given the Index Number of 100. Each month, then, the average of the prices of the same commodities is compared with the standard, and it is in this way easy to follow a general rise or fall in the price level. If we turn to the figures published by *The Times* on March 1, 1932, we shall find that for the month of February the Index Number for food stood at 110·3, and for materials at 94, while taking food and material together, the Index Number for the whole 60 commodities was 100, or exactly the same as the average for the year 1913.

Changes in the general price level may arise either from some particular commodity, or from a general cause such as an increase or diminution of the purchasing power of the community as a whole. As examples of a particular cause, let us take one or two instances of changes in the conditions of supply to the English market. It is easily seen that a bad harvest in the big grain-producing countries of the world would tend to bring about an increase in the price of wheat and flour, and that a failure in the cotton crop is almost sure to result in a rise in the price of raw cotton, cotton thread, and cotton cloth. Similarly, we might expect that if it so happened that there were made available new sources of supply of any food product or raw material it would tend to bring down the prices of those commodities. Any of these changes in the conditions of supply of individual commodities would naturally affect not only their own price in the market, but the average price of commodities as a whole, and so it would be reflected in the Index Number.

It has just been pointed out that the price level for February, 1932, was practically the same as that for the year 1913; but we must not suppose that in the interval between those two dates the price level remained even approximately the same. During the war everything became dearer, partly due to the scarcity of essential commodities, and partly to the increase in currency which took place as an outcome of war conditions; and after the war prices mounted still higher, reaching a culminating point in 1920, when the Board of Trade Index Number for wholesale prices stood as high as 307. Since that time, owing primarily to a policy of deflation, or gradual reduction in the amount of the circulating medium, prices have steadily fallen, a movement accelerated at a later date by general trade depression. This downward movement has not been confined to this country, the fall in the wholesale prices of commodities generally being practically world-wide. As this fall in prices has not in this country at any rate been accompanied by a corresponding fall in costs of production and more especially in rates of wages, it has meant that industry has tended to become unprofitable, that business incomes generally have been on the whole considerably reduced and that there has also been a great and widespread increase of unemployment. One consequence of this was the setting up in November of 1929 of a Government Committee, under the chairmanship of Lord Macmillan, to investigate the causes of this depression, more especially from the point of view of banking, finance, and credit, and to recommend such measures as would enable the financial machinery to assist in the development of trade and commerce and to promote employment of labour. The Report of the Macmillan Committee was issed in July of 1931, just at the time when the seriousness of the financial position was becoming generally recognized. Space will not permit more than a very brief reference to the conclusions arrived at by the Committee and to the recommendations made on the strength of them.

THE MACMILLAN REPORT

In the first place, it is stated in the Report that the great problem of unemployment is definitely connected with monetary policy. The return to a Gold Standard in 1925 involved a rise in the value of sterling, that is to say, a fall in the general level of prices, but costs of production generally did not adapt themselves to the new conditions, with the result that the prices prevailing did not suffice to cover these costs with a reasonable margin of profit. Hence there was much unemployment and acute general depression, the latter both a cause and a result of the former. The question of prices was in the main one of monetary policy, hence with monetary policy the investigation was more particularly concerned. To a rise in prices the Committee looked for a return of prosperity to trade and industry, for a general stimulation of business activity and for a decrease in the amount of unemployment; while increased demand for labour would improve the working class income, which in its turn would increase purchasing power and so help to maintain the improved conditions. The prime object then of international statesmanship, the Report pointed out, should be to attain a new level of prices and having achieved it to maintain it at that point with the greatest possible degree of stability.

This brings us back to the subject of the present chapter, viz. the Bank of England. The desired result was to be obtained as the outcome of an improved monetary system, and as regards this country, the instrument for working it was to be the Bank of England—"an excellent instrument for the purpose; independent of political influences, yet functioning solely in the public interest; with long traditions and experience and clothed with vast prestige, yet not distrustful of evolutionary change or hesitant of new responsibility".

The Bank of England was to work in close co-operation with the Central Banks of other countries, and price stability was to be accomplished through a unified control of gold movements and through the maintenance of such gold reserves as should be able effectively to support a currency and credit system equal to the task of meeting trade requirements without either shortage or excess.

With regard to the question of note issue, the Report pronounced in favour of greater elasticity. It regarded the provisions of the Act of 1928 referred to above as unsatisfactory, for with a fixed fiduciary issue every export of gold meant a reduction of currency. To improve this it was recommended:

(1) That the Bank of England should be allowed to reckon any balances it might hold with the Bank for International Settlements as coming within the meaning of the term "Reserves".

(2) That the active circulation (i.e. total issue less those held as Reserve by the Bank) should be normally £380 millions, with a fixed limit of £400 millions. Treasury authorization to be required for amounts temporarily needed in excess of this.

(3) That the Bank should as a rule keep a larger gold reserve, fluctuating between £100 millions and £175 millions, and supplemented to the extent of a further amount of £50 millions by balances kept with Central Banks of other countries and the Bank for International Settlements.

The recommendations of the Report as regards the monetary policy of the Bank of England may be summed up very briefly as being greater elasticity, greater freedom and greater liquidity.

The final conclusion which the Committee arrived at in their Report was that it was desirable that "we should maintain the gold standard at its present parity". Yet within two months of its publication we had already been forced "off gold" and there seems to be no likelihood whatever of our returning to it "at its present parity". All the same the value of the Report as a whole is undiminished and the three recommendations summarized above may be regarded as a real contribution towards the solution of a very difficult problem.

THE GOLD RESERVE

A very important function of the Bank of England is that of regulating the Gold Reserve. As already pointed out, the Gold Reserve is kept in the Issue Department. It can only be increased by the Bank's giving out additional notes in exchange for new gold brought in, and diminished by its giving out gold in exchange for notes, which when brought back are destroyed. In other words, the Reserve is increased when the Bank is a buyer of gold and diminished when it is a seller.

Gold may be purchased by the Bank either through the compulsory clause in the Bank Charter Act of 1844, or by going as a buyer into the open market. This Act states that "All persons shall be entitled to demand from the Issue Department of the Bank of England Bank of England Notes in exchange for Gold Bullion at the Rate of Three Pounds Seventeen Shillings and Ninepence per Ounce of Standard Gold".[1] The price thus being fixed, it may readily be seen that people would only sell their gold to the Bank when the market price of gold was not above this price. Standard gold being eleven parts of fine gold to one of alloy, this would mean that a market price of £4. 5s. per ounce of fine gold would be about the limit above which gold would not be taken to the Bank for sale under this section of the Act.

Considering that almost ever since Great Britain went off the Gold Standard the price of gold in the open market has been far in excess of this figure, for the most part in fact in the neighbourhood of £6 an ounce, it may safely be stated that the Gold Reserve of the Bank of England has not been increased to any extent from sales to it of this kind.

If then the Bank wants to increase its reserve of gold, it must be by the second of the two methods mentioned above, namely by the purchase of gold in the open market. London is the great gold market of the world; to it is brought for sale

---

[1] Bank Charter Act, 1844, Section IV.

the output of South African, Australian, Canadian and Indian gold mines. When the Bank goes into the market as a purchaser of gold it is in competition with buyers from other countries, that is to say, countries still on the Gold Standard, and consequently it has to pay the market price, whatever that may happen to be. This being the case, it may be assumed that it would only be in very special circumstances, such as for example when pursuing a deliberate policy of increasing the Gold Reserve, that the Bank would be likely to make purchases in this way.

As regards the sale of gold, this can hardly be said to be a matter of practical importance so long as the country remains off the Gold Standard. Since September, 1931, it has not been possible for anyone to demand gold from the Bank in exchange for notes, and it is hardly likely that the Bank would of its own accord sell any of the gold it held in reserve unless it were to meet some special emergency such as occurred in December, 1932, when gold was required by the Government for payment of the instalment of the War Debt then due to the United States of America.

THE BANK RATE

While we were still on the Gold Standard the Gold Reserve was increased or decreased from time to time as a result of any external influence which tended to bring about an inflow or outflow of gold. Of such influences the outstanding examples would be the international movements of capital which are continually taking place, and the payments in one direction or the other arising out of the balance of international indebtedness.

On this inflow and outflow of gold the Bank of England was able to exercise a certain amount of influence through the employment of an instrument which was ready to its hand, namely, the Bank Rate. This is the official minimum rate at which the Bank is willing to discount bills or to make advances to its customers. Changes in the Bank Rate may take place without any reference whatever to the movements of gold: they may merely have to do with the state of the Money Market at the particular moment. The official rate fixed by the Bank of England exercises an important influence on rates of interest charged by the joint stock banks and other suppliers of money, and when raising or lowering the rate it takes into account the general redundancy or scarcity of loanable money at the time. When money for loans is in plentiful supply the rate may be lowered in order to tempt business people generally to borrow more; when it is scarce the rate may be raised in order to check the demand for loans.

This, however, is quite apart from using the Bank Rate as a means of regulating the Gold Reserve by attracting gold when more is wanted and by reducing the existing stock when it is in excess of what is required. It is easy to understand that if the Bank Rate in London were lower than that in other great financial centres, the normal tendency would be for money to be withdrawn from this country and deposited in countries where a higher rate of interest could be obtained for it, and contrariwise, that if the English Bank Rate were higher than in other countries foreigners would be led to deposit their money in London.

When the Bank of England was buying and selling gold freely, a portion at any rate of this international money would have taken the form of gold and have found its way in or out of the Bank of England as the case might be. If the Bank wanted to check a drain of gold it raised the rate, if it wanted to encourage the withdrawal of gold it lowered the rate, and in this way the Gold Reserve was maintained at the level aimed at by the Directors of the Bank.

In this connection it is instructive to follow the changes which have taken place in the Gold Reserve since the crisis of 1931. At the time of our going off the Gold Standard the Gold Reserve was approximately £120 millions. It continued

for some months at about this figure, until, in fact, in anticipation of the payment to America of the instalment of War
Debt due on December 15, 1932, the Bank gradually began
to increase this amount by purchasing gold from time to time.

As a result of these purchases the situation was that after,
on December 15, selling to the Treasury gold to the value of
£19,632,831 for the purpose of this December payment,
the Gold Reserve was again back at about the £120 millions
figure. Soon after this, however, an increase again became
noticeable, and by the end of February, 1933, the Bank had,
as the result of a number of gold purchases, amounting in all
to nearly £28 millions, brought the Gold Reserve up to about
£148 millions, or to a very much better position even than
that it was in prior to December 15.

These purchases continued throughout the month of
March and as a consequence the Bank return for April 5,
1933 (the first to show the return of the fiduciary issue to the
legal figure of £260 millions) gives a Gold Reserve of
£176,532,791. In the absence of any official statement by
the Bank as to the reasons for these purchases it would be
hazardous to attempt to put forward any explanation of them.
It may, however, be permissible to suggest that the Bank's
policy in increasing the Gold Reserve at this time is definitely
connected with the fact that renewed confidence abroad in
the financial stability of Great Britain has led to a considerable
demand for sterling in foreign countries, with the natural
result that the value of the pound has taken an upward
direction, thus facilitating the purchase of gold.

REDUCTION IN THE FIDUCIARY ISSUE

As the reduction in the fiduciary issue was accomplished
by the Issue Department's selling securities to the value of
£15 millions to the Banking Department and obtaining from
it a corresponding amount of notes for cancellation, the returns of both departments were affected by this transaction.

For purposes of comparison the Bank return for April 5, 1933, is given at the end of this chapter. It will be noticed that the principal differences between this and the return given on pp. 155–56 are:

In the Issue Department:

(1) There is a considerable increase in the total note issue following upon the purchases of gold, notwithstanding the fact that the fiduciary issue has been reduced by £15 millions.

(2) The Gold Reserve has been increased by nearly £56 millions.

(3) Other Government securities are down by about £15 millions owing to the sale to the Banking Department.

In the Banking Department:

(4) Bankers deposits are very much higher.

(5) Government securities show a considerable increase, part of which is due to the purchase recorded above.

(6) Other securities are very much lower, but it will be noticed that Government securities have taken their place.

(7) The reserve of notes is larger than in February, 1932, though it is about £15 millions less than it was on March 29.

(8) The proportion of Reserve to Deposits, which on February 17, 1932, was 44 %, is about $41\frac{1}{2}$%.

The question of the gold reserve and how it is affected by the movement of gold from one centre to another is very closely bound up with that of the maintenance of the Gold Standard, and hence its further consideration may conveniently be left to another chapter in which the financial crisis of 1931 and its consequences are dealt with at some length.

BANK OF ENGLAND RETURN

April 5, 1933

Issue Department

Dr.			Cr.	
Notes issued:			Government debt ...	£11,015,100
In circulation ...	£371,669,360		Other Government securities	236,317,844
In Banking Department	64,863,431		Other securities ...	9,024,341
			Silver coin	3,642,715
			Amount of fiduciary issue	£260,000,000
			Gold coin and bullion	176,532,791
	£436,532,791			£436,532,791

Banking Department

Dr.			Cr.	
Capital	£14,553,000		Government securities	£82,979,505
Rest	3,101,705		Other securities:	
Public deposits[1] ...	14,082,962		Discounts and advances	11,648,718
Other deposits:			Securities	15,517,287
Bankers	109,598,886		Notes	64,863,431
Other accounts ...	34,495,482		Gold and silver coin...	827,614
Seven-day and other bills...	4,520			
	£175,836,555			£175,836,555

[1] Including Exchequer, Savings Banks, Commissioners of National Debt and Dividend accounts.

CHAPTER XII

THE FINANCIAL CRISIS OF 1931 AND THE GOLD STANDARD

The outstanding political event of 1931 was the establishment of a National Government including in its ranks members of all three great political parties, Conservative, Liberal and Labour, and taking the place of the Labour Government which had held office since the General Election of May, 1929.

This political change, which had its origin in the grave state of affairs financially then existing, took place suddenly and unexpectedly in the month of August. For some time it had been quite evident that the situation was far from satisfactory. There was every reason to think that there would be a serious budget deficit for the year ending April, 1932, and for months past the Board of Trade returns had been showing that the gap between imports and exports was steadily widening, with the consequence that the Balance of Trade was becoming more and more unfavourable.

These monthly returns, however, could not present the whole of the picture, for they only contained the figures of what are called "visible imports and exports"—that is to say, of actual merchandise passing in and out of the country. If the necessary material had been available, it would have revealed a state of things that was only suspected, viz. that the "invisible exports" which were relied upon to counterbalance the excess of imports over exports had themselves fallen off to such an extent that the state of things was much worse than had been generally realized. By "invisible exports" is meant all the various services rendered to people abroad for which payment would have to be made, the chief of which are Banking and Insurance services, shipping freights, the use of capital invested abroad, and the expenditure in the country of foreign travellers.

The anxiety that was being felt found expression in the House of Commons already in February, 1931, when the Conservative Opposition moved a vote of censure on the Government for its policy of adding to the national expenditure at a time when revenue was falling off and there was urgent need for economy. The motion was not carried, but there was general support for a Liberal amendment to the effect that an independent committee should be set up for the purpose of investigating the country's financial position. As a result of this a committee was formed in the following month, to be known as the Committee of National Expenditure, which, under the Chairmanship of Sir George May, was to conduct a thorough inquiry into the matter, and make such recommendations as it might think necessary for the solution of the problem. The terms of reference of this Committee were as follows:

To make recommendations to the Chancellor of the Exchequer for effecting forthwith all possible reductions in the National Expenditure on Supply Services, having regard especially to the present and prospective position of the Revenue. In so far as questions of policy are involved in the expenditure under discussion, these will remain for the exclusive consideration of the Cabinet; but it will be open to the Committee to review the expenditure and to indicate the economies which might be effected if particular policies were either adopted, abandoned or modified.

The Report of this Committee was issued on July 31. It pointed out that there would be a budget deficit in the current year of some £120 millions and of a still larger sum in the year following.

We fear (said the Report) that the country must face the disagreeable fact that the public expenditure—and in this we include local as well as national expenditure—is too high, and that it must be brought down to a lower level.

To meet this situation economies were recommended, including a "cut in the unemployment dole". It was on this particular question that the split in the Labour Party occurred which led to Mr Ramsay MacDonald's resignation and to his being entrusted by His Majesty the King "with the task of forming a national government on a comprehensive basis for the purpose of meeting the present financial emergency". This form of words made it abundantly clear that the emergency which had arisen was a financial one and that the new Government was formed for the purpose of introducing such measures as would tend to bring the country back to a position of financial stability. The task before the new Government was clearly set out in the announcement which on August 24 followed immediately upon its appointment:

In order to correct without delay the excess of national expenditure over revenue, it is anticipated that Parliament will be summoned to meet on September 8, when proposals will be submitted to the House of Commons for a very large reduction of expenditure and for the provision on an equitable basis of the further funds required to balance the Budget. As the commerce and well-being, not only of the British nation, but of a large part of the civilized world, has been built up and rests upon a well-founded confidence in sterling, the new Government will take whatever steps may be deemed by them to be necessary to justify the maintenance of that confidence unimpaired.

From this it is abundantly clear that to restore confidence in the pound sterling was the special task to which the new Government was pledged to devote itself, and for this two things were immediately necessary: the Budget must be made to balance, and the Balance of Trade must be restored. The former part of the task was taken in hand without any delay and measures were introduced reducing expenditure in many directions and making various additions to taxation. To quote the Chancellor of the Exchequer speaking in the House of Commons on September 10:

Drastic and disagreeable measures will have to be taken; large economies are essential and so are heavy increases of taxation.

It was hoped that these measures would suffice to restore the confidence of people generally, both in this country and abroad, but such was not the case; heavy withdrawals of gold continued, and on September 20 the Government had to announce that the country had been forced to abandon the Gold Standard.

THE GOLD STANDARD

That there was a serious loss of confidence in the stability of the pound sterling was evident already some few weeks before the publication of the "May Report", for in the middle of July there commenced a considerable drain of gold from the Bank of England. To some extent no doubt this was due to nervousness on the part of British subjects, but the "flight from the pound" was in the main caused by loss of confidence on the part of foreign depositors, who began in haste to withdraw their money from the country. This drain of gold was in effect so heavy as to threaten to drive us off the Gold Standard to which we had returned so recently as 1925, and it was this danger which evidently the Government had before it in making the pronouncement quoted above.

The situation becomes clearer if we bear in mind the financial history of those few critical weeks prior to Mr MacDonald's resignation on August 24.[1]

> On July 9 the Bank's reserve of gold was £166 millions, a figure somewhat above the normal.
> On July 16 it was £165 millions, a very slight difference.
> On July 23 it was £150 millions, a fall of 15 millions.
> On July 30 it was £133 millions, a fall of 17 millions more.

To check this drain of gold the Bank had on July 23 resorted to the usual method of protecting its reserve and had

---

[1] The figures quoted were given on p. 162, but for the reader's convenience they are set out again here.

raised the official rate from $2\frac{1}{2}\%$ to $3\frac{1}{2}\%$. This not having the desired effect, a week later the rate was again raised from $3\frac{1}{2}\%$ to $4\frac{1}{2}\%$, but still the drain went on. The Bank had now resort to borrowing, for credits abroad would do away with the necessity of exporting gold, and it was able to announce on August 1 that the Bank of France and the Federal Reserve Bank of New York had each placed at the disposal of the Bank a credit for £25 millions or £50 millions in all. At the same time the Treasury, as mentioned before, authorized the Bank to raise the fiduciary note issue for a period of three weeks from £260 millions to £275 millions. On the expiration of this period the authorization was renewed for another three months and by further extensions it continued to remain operative until March 31, 1933, when it was allowed to lapse. In four weeks' time these French and American credits were exhausted and fresh borrowing took place. This time it was the Treasury that took the necessary steps and it obtained from the financial authorities in New York and Paris further credit facilities amounting to £80 millions in all. On September 21, Mr Snowden, as he then was,[1] informed the House of Commons that no less than £200 millions had already been withdrawn from this country. He did not state specifically where this immense sum had come from, but we may assume that it was made up in the following way:

The £33 millions of gold withdrawn in July.
The £130 millions of French and American credits,
    and some £37 millions from various assets of the Bank in
    the form of other credits and foreign currency holdings.

Two hundred millions had been withdrawn, but there were still in this country large balances kept by foreigners with the various banks, which, as Mr Snowden said, largely exceeded in amount the Bank of England's entire reserve of

[1] Mr Snowden was raised to the Peerage in November, 1931, and took the title of Viscount Snowden.

gold and which were liable to be withdrawn at any time. Hence there was nothing for it but to suspend the Gold Standard Act of 1925, and for the Bank to be relieved of its obligation to sell gold in exchange for notes. The terms of this obligation were, it will be remembered, set out in Chapter IX, so it is unnecessary to say more about them here.[1]

It may be useful before going further to consider the circumstances under which a drain of gold is liable to arise. In the first place a drain of gold may be internal or external. It would be internal if the withdrawal were made by those living in the country acting possibly either under the influence of panic or in that state of nervous uncertainty which is induced when owing to inflation the currency undergoes a rapid depreciation. It would be external if the withdrawal were made by foreigners who, owing to a financial crisis in their own country, needed their money at home, or who had lost confidence in the financial position of the country where their money was deposited.

The drain was certainly an internal one in 1797, when so great was the apprehension caused by the attempted French invasion of the previous year, that there was a run on the Bank of England, and the Government found it necessary to issue an order suspending the obligation of the Bank to redeem its notes in gold coin. In 1931, on the contrary, the drain was for the most part external, though there was doubtless a certain amount of gold demanded from the Bank by nervous people at home who thought their money would be safer abroad, but "flight from the pound" from this direction did not reach any very great dimensions, and it may safely be asserted that withdrawals were in the main due to the loss of confidence abroad due to the bad impression created by what had become known of our financial, political and industrial difficulties. We must, however, not lose sight of the fact that there was at the time a very serious financial strin-

[1] See Chapter IX, p. 132.

gency in many foreign centres in consequence of which, even if there had not been this loss of confidence in the pound sterling, bankers abroad would in any case have most likely withdrawn a part, if not the whole, of their London deposits to meet the claims which were being made upon themselves.

Thus there seem to be very good grounds for the statement so often made that the drain of gold, and the subsequent depreciation of sterling, were due to external rather than internal causes and that we did not voluntarily abandon the Gold Standard but were so to speak driven off it.

Much difference of opinion has been expressed in business and other circles as to whether we were right in returning to the Gold Standard in 1925, and also as to whether there is any advantage to be gained from being on the Gold Standard at any time. Those opposed to the system expressed great satisfaction at our having been forced to abandon it, and their hope and expectation is that we shall never again return to it. Others take quite an opposite view, they regard our departure from the system as a misfortune that could not be avoided and they look forward to a return to it when the conditions of international trade and finance are sufficiently normal to justify such a step. But this controversy is quite outside the scope of the present work and hence no reference can be made to the respective views of the opposing parties. It is, however, well within our limits to inquire what difference coming off the Gold Standard has made to this country, and this inquiry will be simplified if in the first instance we set out very briefly the part played by gold in the business life of the community generally.

THE FUNCTIONS OF GOLD

The four chief functions of gold may be briefly set out as follows:

(1) Gold is the measure of values, that is to say, with it we are able to compare the values of all other things. We

measure values by referring them to the unit of currency; in this country the pound, in the United States of America the dollar, in France the franc, in Germany the mark, and each of these units is considered to represent a certain fixed amount of gold. This makes possible a basis of comparison between the currencies of different countries and consequently between the prices of commodities in different countries, since they are all referred to the same measure, namely, a certain weight of gold. When Great Britain was on the Gold Standard we were able to say that when the exchanges were at par, one pound was equal to 4·86⅔ dollars or 124·21 francs or 40·43 marks, because all these represented the same amount of fine gold, namely 113 grains, or its equivalent of slightly less than 8 grammes.

(2) The Gold Reserve of the central bank of a country is the basis of its currency and credit. The amount of currency issued, and the amount of credit allowed by banks to their customers depend in the last resort on the amount of this gold reserve. Further, owing to its control over the volume of currency and credit, that is in effect over the amount of purchasing power available in the country at any given time, gold exercises a definite influence on the general level of prices.

(3) Gold provides an alternative method of payment in international trade. What a country imports may be paid for either in goods and services or in gold and in no other way. If a country imports more than it exports, and these terms must be understood to include what are known as invisible imports and exports, such as the services of capital invested in another country, services of shipping, and insurance, money expended by foreign visitors, etc., the surplus of imports over exports must be paid for in gold which really in such

cases amounts to the export of gold to the amount of the balance that has not been adjusted in any other way.

(4) In addition to maintaining a balance between exports and imports, gold tends to bring the price levels of different countries into line with one another. This follows from the effect which the amount of gold reserve in the central bank of the country has on the general level of prices. When gold is withdrawn currency and credit are restricted and prices generally within the country tend to fall. The result of the lower price level is that foreign buyers are attracted, that exports increase, that the balance of trade is redressed, and if exports now exceed imports gold comes back. So long, therefore, as gold was free to pass unchecked from one country to another, adjusting in this way the balance of international trade, the action just described tended to be almost automatic; but countries off the Gold Standard have placed an embargo on the export of gold, and some of those that have remained on it have imposed restrictions on its transfer abroad, and hence this balancing function of gold is to a very large extent in suspense.

We are now in a better position to consider the question as to what difference going off the Gold Standard has made to Great Britain, more especially in this same matter of the various functions of gold which we have just been examining.

(1) As regards gold being taken as the measure of values, we are still able to say that the pound is the measure to which all values are referred, and that internally it may still retain its full value, that is, its purchasing power, provided that there is no inflation of the purchasing medium whether currency or credit; but the one pound note can no longer purchase 113 grains of fine gold, nor can it purchase the same amount as

before of the currencies of those countries which are
still on the Gold Standard, and because it can purchase
less of some other currencies, it can also purchase less
in the way of the goods or services which have to be
paid for in those currencies, for it is by purchasing the
currency of a country that we are able to pay for the
goods and services with which that country has supplied us.

(2) Gold is still the basis of currency and credit in this
country, for both bear a relation to the amount of gold
reserve. Moreover, the connection which exists between the volume of currency and credit on the one
hand and the general level of prices on the other is
undisturbed by the fact that the Gold Standard has
been abandoned, though any expansion of the circulating medium would, unless accompanied by an
increase in gold reserve, have to be met by an increase
in the fiduciary issue. In this case the gold reserve
would be supporting a larger superstructure of currency
and credit, or, in other words, there would be an
economization of gold.

(3) Gold no longer provides an alternative method of payment, because the Bank of England which holds the
reserve of gold has ceased to part with it in exchange
for notes. Gold could of course be purchased in the
open market, but its high price would make its use as
a method of payment quite out of the question. The
only way, therefore, in which we can transfer money
abroad either for the purpose of paying for goods or of
making loans or of meeting any other financial obligations is by purchasing foreign currency, and the amount
of that foreign currency which we can purchase depends
to a large extent on the willingness of the foreigner to
take our currency in exchange for his. This willingness

to take our currency is influenced by two main considerations:

(*a*) How much he can buy with it in this country, or, in other words, the general level of prices here;

and   (*b*) His feeling of confidence in the stability of the pound sterling, that is, in the maintenance of its value as expressed in terms of other currencies.

(4) As gold is no longer passing freely from country to country from centres where it has less purchasing power to others where it has greater, it has ceased to function as the equilibrating influence between currencies, which makes them conform within narrow limits to the par of exchange. The anchor which kept the pound sterling fast to the dollar, the franc, or the mark, has been lost, and hence, there may be from day to day wide fluctuations in the rates of foreign exchange or, to put it in other words, the value of the pound as expressed in foreign currencies is not a comparatively fixed or stable one, but is decided by the conditions of supply and demand prevailing in the money market at the particular moment.

THE VALUE OF THE POUND

In this discussion we have for the most part been using the term "the value of the pound" in a very special sense, namely its value as expressed in terms of the currencies of other countries, but this is not the only or in fact the ordinary sense in which the term is used. The value of the pound usually means its purchasing power, and that value is said to be more or less according as the general price level is lower or higher, that is to say when prices are lower more can be purchased with a one pound note and hence the pound may be said to have a higher value, and contrariwise when prices are higher less can be purchased with a pound note and the pound has consequently a lower value. In foreign trade, however, the difference between the value of the pound as expressed in its power to purchase commodities, and in its power to purchase foreign currencies, is apparent rather than real, for the value of those foreign currencies to anyone purchasing them depends on the level of prices in the particular foreign country, and it is evident that the less a pound can buy of, say, German marks, the less it can buy of German goods.

We arrive, therefore, at two values of the pound sterling which we may call at once its internal and external values, namely what it can purchase at home and what it can purchase abroad. When countries are on the Gold Standard the rates of exchange tend, as has already been shown, to deviate comparatively little from the normal point represented by the par of exchange. Under these circumstances the internal and external values of the currency are practically the same, but when a country is off the Gold Standard there may be wide differences between the internal and external values of its currency, and this is especially the case when the other country in question is still adhering to the Gold Standard system. The financial history of Germany in the years immediately following the war provides us with a very good example of the wide difference that may exist between the internal and external values of the currency. The value of the mark had fallen at home, for prices were very much higher than the pre-war level, but it had fallen far more abroad, for it could purchase a very much less quantity of foreign currency which, as shown above, is the same thing as saying it would purchase far less than before of other countries' goods. To give a concrete example: in January of 1922, the rate of exchange between Germany and Great Britain fluctuated round about 400 marks to the pound, that is to say its value externally was about $\frac{1}{20}$ of the normal. On the other hand, the price level in Germany was about five times the pre-war level, hence, the mark internally had only a purchasing power of $\frac{1}{5}$. From this it will be seen that at that particular time the internal value of the mark was about four times that of its external value.

Since Great Britain went off the Gold Standard a similar discrepancy has arisen, though to a far less marked degree. The value of the pound at home has undergone practically no variation. There has been no inflation of the currency, and there has been very little change in the price level, but the external value of the pound has fallen appreciably, at one time rather more than 30%, and this means that when there was this amount of depreciation, though we were paying very much the same for what we bought at home, we had to pay some 30% more for what we bought abroad, that is of course assuming that such purchases were made in countries still on the Gold Standard. In countries which like ourselves have gone off the Gold Standard, the pound has retained very much the same value as it had before and in some cases it has even a higher value. Our commercial relations with them have thus been comparatively little affected by this currency question. It is clear then that a country which is no longer on the Gold Standard is at a disadvantage as regards its imports from Gold Standard countries, inasmuch as it has to pay for them with a depreciated pound, but against this must be set the corresponding advantage which it has on its exports. It is quite a common saying that a depreciated currency offers a bonus to exporters. This is very easily explained, for the foreign importer has to buy currency of the country from which the goods come in order to pay for them, and, as has been the case since September, 1931, he has had to pay less for the pound sterling than before. Thus since the prices of goods in Great Britain have remained practically the same he has been able to get what he has bought more cheaply. For the same reason it is clear that there is an inducement to a German merchant to buy British goods in preference, say, to French or American, and thus, while our imports are likely to decrease, owing to the fact that they are costing us more, our exports are likely to increase, because the foreign buyer can get them for less.

How is it, it may well be asked, that the external value of the pound has fallen in this way? To answer this question we must fall back on the well-known economic proposition that the value of anything depends on the interaction of the forces working behind demand and supply. This applies just as much to money as to goods or services. In either case demand comes from the buyers and supply comes from the sellers. The forces behind demand and supply are the particular reasons which at any given time would induce people to buy or sell as the case may be. Those who buy and sell the currency of any country may do so either for trade reasons or for reasons of finance or, in other words, because either they may have to pay or receive money for goods bought or sold, or they may want to transfer money to another country and to deposit it there for reasons of security. Passing from the general to the particular, we may regard the foreign merchant who has bought goods in this country as a buyer of English currency to pay for them. The foreign banker, too, who wants to deposit money in England must buy pounds sterling to enable him to do so. Similarly, the Englishman buying goods abroad or placing money in a foreign centre must sell English currency in order to carry out either transaction. Where there are more buyers than sellers of sterling the value of sterling rises and, vice versa, where there are more sellers than buyers its value falls. Before we went off the Gold Standard a fall could be prevented by shipments of gold, but at a time when gold is no longer to be obtained from the Bank of England for export there is nothing to prevent the value of the pound falling to that level at which buyers are willing to take what sellers are ready to dispose of, for, according to the law of value, a fall in prices tempts more buyers, and a rise in prices tempts more sellers, until a point of equilibrium between buyers and sellers is reached which we call the market price.

The fall in the value of the pound, therefore, can be easily accounted for. In the first place the balance of trade has been and still is against us; we are importing more than we export, and even when we take into account the invisible exports referred to above, that is, the services we render through our shipping, capital invested abroad, and in various other ways, it is estimated that the trade returns of the year 1933 will still show an adverse balance in spite of the efforts made to bring about an equilibrium. This means that until we are able to strike a balance between exports and imports we must expect to find that there are more sellers than buyers of sterling for the purposes of foreign trade. In the second place, on the financial side, as has already been pointed out, the want of confidence in sterling led to the withdrawal of money deposited in this country. This again meant selling of sterling, and it is this excess of selling over buying which brought the external value of the pound at one time as low as between 13s. and 14s. This state of things, however, is not by any means necessarily permanent, for

(1) If through the measures taken to check imports and through the encouragement afforded to exports, the balance of trade should once again become favourable, buyers of sterling for trade purposes would outnumber the sellers and the value of the pound would accordingly tend to rise.

(2) If in foreign centres generally there should be a return of confidence in England's financial stability, instead of the withdrawal of deposits we are likely to see some return of deposits already withdrawn. If this should be the case there would again be from this source a demand for sterling which would tend to send its value up again.

The great thing to be aimed at, therefore, is the removal of the causes of depreciation by adjusting the balance of trade, by showing the world that measures have been taken to secure a balanced Budget, and lastly, by carrying out a financial policy which will command complete confidence abroad.

WAS GOING OFF THE GOLD STANDARD NECESSARY?

Some foreign critics have expressed the opinion that there would have been no necessity for our going off the Gold Standard if the Bank of England had adopted in time the usual method of checking a drain of gold, that is, by raising to a sufficiently high figure the official bank rate. At the end of the previous chapter it was pointed out that when a country is on the Gold Standard and gold can be obtained freely in exchange for notes, the bank rate is a very effective instrument for regulating the gold reserve of the Bank, for by lowering the rate foreigners are as a rule induced to borrow, and by raising it borrowers are discouraged while, at the same time, money is attracted to the country owing to the higher rate of interest that can be obtained for its use. In order to answer the above criticism we must carry the subject a little further and consider why, under the circumstances prevailing in August and September of 1931, raising the bank rate would not have been likely to accomplish its purpose of stopping the drain of gold. As already pointed out, the rate was raised on July 23 from $2\frac{1}{2}$ to $3\frac{1}{2}\%$ and on July 30 from $3\frac{1}{2}$ to $4\frac{1}{2}\%$, and that these changes failed to have the desired effect or, in other words, gold continued to be withdrawn in very large quantities. We must distinguish between movements of gold under normal trade conditions and such movements as may be the result of panic or uncertainty. Let us take the normal movements first and consider again the function of gold in establishing a balance between exports and imports. Where there is free movement of gold the tendency is for it always to go to those countries where its value is highest, that is, where prices are lowest or where loanable capital earns the highest reward. Left to itself gold like water will tend to find its own level, but the flow of gold is seldom allowed to be entirely automatic, for during the period which might elapse between a heavy withdrawal of gold and its return later owing to the fall of prices that that withdrawal has caused, serious results might be experienced. This automatic movement of gold with its alternating inflow and outflow leads to fluctuations—and sometimes very large fluctuations—in the volume of currency and credit, and consequently in the general level of prices. This has a very disorganizing effect on trade and industry and hence the central banks intervene, exercising through changes in the bank rate some control over these gold movements by assisting them at one time and checking them at another.

In time of panic, however, when there is a general want of confidence, the considerations which influence action in normal times fail to have their effect. A higher rate of interest attracts money when at the same time it is felt that the capital sum is not likely to lose any of its value, but when, as happened in July, 1931, there is uncertainty about the stability or security of the money itself, even a considerable rise in the bank rate would fail to bring in new money or to stop the withdrawal of that already deposited.

CHAPTER XIII

SOME ASPECTS OF INTERNATIONAL TRADE

The two subjects of Finance and International Trade are so closely bound up together that it is difficult to deal with them in separate chapters without a certain amount of overlapping. This applies with special force to such matters as the Balance of Trade and the Foreign Exchanges, to both of which reference has from time to time been made in connection with Banking and the Gold Standard. Under the heading "Some Aspects of International Trade", these two questions will again be discussed, but in their case, as throughout the whole chapter, an attempt will be made to emphasize as much as possible the trading point of view.

HISTORICAL OUTLINE

Foreign, or, to use the more expressive term, International Trade is the natural outcome of the expansion of human wants beyond what it is in the power of national resources to supply. From very early times it has invariably happened that when the inhabitants of one country have come into contact with those of another, they have at once mutually recognized that there are marked differences in their respective modes of life. They may not be using, for example, the same kinds of food, clothing, ornament or weapons of defence. These differences give rise to a desire to possess the things which have roused their interest, and these possibly are not to be made in the homeland because the soil and climate may not be suitable for their production, the necessary mineral deposits may not exist and the industrial arts may not be sufficiently advanced. This leads in the first instance no doubt to some exchange of products between them, and before long there develops a more or less regular commercial intercourse.

Early examples of international trade can be found in the early economic history of Great Britain. Even before the Christian Era there seems to have been an active export of tin from Cornwall, and in Roman times British corn, cattle, hides, metals, furs and slaves were being sent to Rome and other parts of the Roman Empire in exchange for the many different articles of daily use, luxuries as well as necessaries, with which the Britons had become familiar under the Roman occupation.

At a later date, first the Norman Conquest, then the Crusades, brought many new ideas into English social life and led to the adoption of a new standard of living generally. The wants thus stimulated could only be satisfied through trade with foreign countries. How otherwise could the mediaeval baron, for example, have obtained the highly finished armour and weapons used by the continental knights, which he had learned to covet when fighting with them in France or in the Holy Land? Or how again could his wife and daughters have secured those delicate tissues of wool, linen and silk, which the continental ladies were in the habit of wearing and which the native craftsmen were not able to produce?

This developing foreign trade gave an immense impetus to English industry, for to obtain foreign products other goods must be produced at home in larger quantities and of a kind for which there was a ready demand in markets abroad. The chief English export at this time was wool, and to produce this in sufficiently large quantities much land was enclosed for sheep farming, and this may be said to have been one of the causes of the breaking up of the Manorial System with its ideal of economic self-sufficiency.

In Plantagenet times this development of foreign trade was greatly encouraged by successive monarchs because it provided them with a very useful additional source of revenue. Foreign merchants came much to England, while

English merchants established themselves in the staple towns of France and Flanders. From this time onwards foreign trade relations developed rapidly, especially under the Tudors, in whose time privileges were secured in foreign markets, commercial treaties were concluded, shipping was encouraged, discoveries were made, and there was even the beginning of colonization.

THE MERCANTILE SYSTEM

From this time also we can date the development of what is known as the Mercantile System, a political system under which it was sought to promote the prosperity of the country, not as an end in itself, but as a means by which a strong national state might be built up, national power secured and national importance increased. National greatness was considered to depend on economic prosperity, and economic prosperity on the extension of foreign commerce, hence the connection thus established between commerce and power gave rise to the term "Mercantile". We find the elements of the Mercantile policy already in the reign of Edward IV, if not still earlier, but it took a much more definite form under Henry VII, of whom Sir Francis Bacon said that "he bowed the policy of England from consideration of plenty to consideration of power".

The Mercantile System may be considered to have dominated English commercial policy for some three centuries, for it is not until the attack made against it by Adam Smith in the latter part of the eighteenth century that it can be said to have lost its hold. Throughout this long period it must not be supposed that there was any uniformity either of policy or of methods. Monarchs and statesmen one after another, while keeping the same general object in view, introduced such measures as the conditions of the day seemed to require. In the earlier part of the period, for example, we have a definite encouragement of the import of the precious metals and in the latter it is clear that the great object was to preserve a favourable balance of trade, the idea being that so long as the balance was in our favour the precious metals would come into the country in the ordinary course of trade. The Mercantilists held the view that the economic activities of the nation should be made to support its political interests, and hence the system is marked by the issuing of a number of regulations and restrictions which, however much they may have contributed towards trade development in its earlier stages, proved a hindrance to that development when trade was rapidly outgrowing the need for such assistance. Hence we get writers like Adam Smith attacking the system and pleading for complete freedom of trade.

The general policy of the Mercantilists may be fairly well indicated by the following diagrammatic statement:

THE MERCANTILE SYSTEM

aims at securing
NATIONAL POWER
|
requires
ARMED FORCES
|
supported by
TREASURE
|
obtained by
FOREIGN TRADE
|
involves
fostering care for

MARKETS	INDUSTRY	POPULATION
Colonies Trading Currency	Training Employment Policy	Food Supply
Companies		
Navigation Re-coinage	Statute of Poor Law Protection	Corn Laws
Acts	Artificers	

The important thing to notice is the connection between the various Legislative Acts and the dominating object of promoting National Power. These Acts may be regarded as parts of a System because they are all related to the definite end in view.

THE THEORY OF INTERNATIONAL TRADE

Under the Free Trade regime, which may be said to date from Gladstone's budget of 1854, though this was merely the climax of a movement which had been gaining strength for some years previously, a very definite theory of International Trade was put forward by economists such as Ricardo and John Stuart Mill. The main contention of those writers was that the forces regulating the terms of exchange in International Trade were essentially different from those which tended to fix prices in home trade, and this view is supported by a much more recent writer, Professor Bastable. Put briefly, their theory is that International Trade is of the nature of barter inasmuch as what a country imports is paid for with what it exports, and that consequently if any hindrance such as Customs Duties are put in the way of the import of foreign goods there will necessarily be a corresponding falling off in export trade. The real problem may be expressed as follows: Considering that in any country exporters and importers are not the same persons and not presumably in touch with one another, how is it possible that the total value of what one set of foreigners buys from us, that is, of our exports, should come to exactly the same figure as the total amount of what we buy from an entirely different set of foreigners, living possibly in quite different parts of the world, that is, of our imports?

The explanation that used to be given was that if a country imported more than it exported the balance had to be paid in gold. The export of gold meant a reduction in the volume of currency in that country and this in turn involved a general lowering of prices, whereas, on the other hand, in the country to which the gold went the currency would be increased and a corresponding rise in prices would follow. The effect of these changes would be an increased demand for the goods of the country with the lower price level and a falling off in the demand for the goods of the country with the higher price level. This would cause the pendulum to swing in the opposite direction; exports now being in excess of imports the gold would have to come back in order to pay for the difference between them. Hence through the movements of gold and their effect first on the currency and then on the price level, exports and imports would tend in the long run to equal one another. But this explanation naturally falls to the ground in the case of countries which have gone off the Gold Standard and from which gold is no longer exported to meet the excess of imports over exports. For such countries, therefore, we must either abandon this theory that in the long run exports must pay for imports, or we must find an explanation independent of gold. Let us examine what this other explanation is.

The starting point is that goods have to be paid for ultimately in the currency of the exporting country, and consequently that with every export there arises a demand from abroad for that currency. But countries import as well as export, and hence there is at any time a demand from abroad for, say, English currency and a demand in England for some foreign currency. Whichever demand happens to be the greater, the value of that currency will tend to rise. If England then were to import more than she exported, the demand in London for foreign currency would be greater than the demand in the foreign country for English currency, and consequently, relatively to that foreign currency, English currency would become of lower value. English currency being cheaper, English goods would to the foreigner also be cheaper, and the demand for them abroad would tend to increase, thus helping to wipe out the surplus of imports over exports. Hence it may be said that through the alteration in the value of the currency which would follow any balance of imports over exports and vice versa, forces would be put into operation which would tend to produce an equilibrium between the two.

The way in which these forces operate in actual business life is explained later on in this chapter in connection with Bills of Exchange.

THE BALANCE OF TRADE

That there would be a tendency towards such equilibrium there is very little doubt, but that it would be the actual state of affairs at any given time would hardly be in accordance with the facts. In the first place there is the assumption that the exports provide the only means of payment for the imports, but this is not the case. In 1913, visible imports were greater than visible exports by £158 millions, but that year invisible exports[1] amounted to some £339 millions, which would turn the balance and leave a surplus in our favour of £181 millions. The £339 millions of invisible exports may be divided into two classes: (1) *earned*, that is, payment for services of shipping, insurance, etc., and (2) *unearned*, that is, interest arising from investments abroad. Of the £339 millions, £129 millions were earned and £210 millions were unearned. Now as the balance against us from actual trade was £158 millions it only needed, in addition to the £129 millions that were *earned*, some £29 millions of the £210 millions received from investments in order to make up the balance. If we deduct these £29 millions from the £210 millions, there will be left £181 millions, the ultimate balance in our favour. Instead of this balance being sent home it was re-invested abroad, and as surpluses of this kind had been occurring for many years past, Great Britain had accumulated

[1] The term "invisible exports" is explained in Chapter XII, p. 183.

an immense amount of capital in various investments in foreign countries. During the war some of these investments had to be sold and in this way the capital of the country was being used to help finance the war.

If we now compare these figures for 1913 with those for 1928 we shall find that the position has changed very unfavourably. In the latter year visible imports exceeded visible exports by some £358 millions. The higher price level prevailing at this time will account for some of the difference but not to such an extent as to hide the fact that the balance of trade had moved considerably against us. In this year invisible exports amounted to £495 millions, of which £225 were earned and £270 unearned, hence to make up the deficit of £358 millions we had to take the whole of the earned amount and £133 millions of the unearned, leaving a balance of £137 millions for re-investment.

The Board of Trade returns for the succeeding years show that the Balance of Trade has been progressively still more unfavourable. The excess of visible imports over visible exports for the years 1929, 1930, 1931 is given as follows:

Year	Excess
	£
1929	381 millions
1930	386 ,,
1931	411 ,,

At the same time the net receipts from invisible exports have rapidly declined, the Board of Trade estimates for the same years being given as follows:

Year	Receipts
	£
1929	484 millions
1930	414 ,,
1931	301 ,,

A comparison of these tables will show that in 1929 the surplus available for fresh investment had fallen to £103 millions, in 1930 to £28 millions and in 1931 there was actually a balance on the wrong side of no less than £110 millions. It was the fear of this adverse balance which, as shown in the last chapter, was one of the causes which led to the large withdrawals of gold and to the United Kingdom being driven off the Gold Standard.

It now becomes clear that so long as it was possible by means of the invisible exports to preserve a favourable Balance of Trade, a condition of fairly stable equilibrium was maintained owing to the fact that the surplus was invested abroad. Since, however, the balance has become unfavourable, and we have ceased to make up the amount by export of gold, the equilibrium has been maintained partly through protective measures which have discouraged imports, partly through the depreciation of our currency which has stimulated exports and at the same time has still further tended to reduce imports, partly, no doubt, by the sale of foreign investments.

DUMPING

In connection with International Trade the question often arises as to whether measures should be taken to discourage, or to prevent altogether, the importation into a country of certain classes of goods, such measures taking the form either of absolute prohibition or of the imposition of specially heavy Customs Duties.

The reason assigned for action of this kind would usually be that the transactions in question are politically, socially or economically undesirable. What is commonly described as "dumping" is a case in point, and as this is a matter of practical importance as well as of general interest it is worth while our considering it in some detail.

What is dumping? A clear definition of the term is certainly needed, for it is often very loosely used, especially when it is brought into discussion of a controversial nature. There is a kind of depreciatory ring about the word itself; it seems to point to something unfair or even discreditable in the particular transaction under consideration. Hence the first thing is to examine somewhat closely what the technical use of the term really is. A view very widely held is that dumped goods are goods offered for sale in a foreign country at a price below that which might be described as economic, that is, below a price which covers the cost of production in the country of origin plus a reasonable percentage of profit. This agrees with the definition given in the Safeguarding of Industries Act of 1921, in which we find dumping defined as "the offer for sale in the United Kingdom of goods manufactured outside at prices below the cost of production". The general idea contained in this definition is quite clear, but the practical application of it leads to a certain amount of confusion. Different manufacturers in the country of origin may have different costs of production and some of them may find it advantageous with a view to keeping their works running to sell their goods abroad at less than the cost of production to them. Yet this price may not be below the cost of production of other manufacturers more fortunately situated as regards manufacturing or distributing costs.

It is perhaps this difficulty of arriving at a standard cost of production in the country from which the goods come that has led to another definition of the term becoming widely recognized. The Canadian Tariff Law of 1907 contains what is known as a "Dumping Clause" in which it is provided that a special duty shall be levied on undervalued goods. The terms of this clause are as follows:

In the case of articles exported to Canada of a class or kind made in Canada, if the export or actual selling price to an importer in Canada be less than the fair market value of the same article when sold for home consumption in the usual and ordinary course in the country whence exported to Canada at the time of its exportation to Canada, there shall, in addition to the duties otherwise established, be levied, collected, and paid on such article on its importation into Canada a special duty (or dumping duty) equal to the difference between the said selling price of the article for export and the said fair market value thereof for home consumption.

From this it is evident, in spite of the somewhat involved wording, that the Canadian Government when inserting this clause regarded the essential feature of "dumping" as being the offering of goods for sale in a foreign country at a lower price than the fair market value of the same goods when they are being offered at home. This definition gets over the difficulty caused by the ambiguity of the term "cost of production" and bases itself on an ascertainable figure, namely, the fair market value, or in other words the current price at which the goods are being actually sold in the country of manufacture.

A third meaning of the term "dumping", quite distinct from either of the two just mentioned, has become prominent in the discussion arising out of the agreements concluded at the Ottawa Conference of 1932. It had been maintained by the Canadian representatives that any system of Empire Preference was in danger of being nullified by wholesale dumping from Russia. As a protection against this danger the following clause was inserted in the Canadian agreement:

This Agreement is made on the express condition that if either Government is satisfied that any preferences hereby granted in respect of any particular class of commodities are likely to be frustrated in whole or in part by reason of the creation or maintenance directly or indirectly of prices for such class of commodities through State action on the part of any foreign country, that Government hereby declares that it will exercise the powers which it now has or will hereafter take to prohibit the entry from such foreign country directly or indirectly of such commodities into its country for such time as may be necessary to make effective and to maintain the preference hereby granted by it.

This involved denunciation of the Commercial Treaty with Russia and Mr J. H. Thomas, when announcing in the House of Commons that the Government had given notice for the termination of the Russian treaty, made use of the following words: "Having entered into an obligation to give preferences within the British Commonwealth of Nations, we must take all necessary steps to see that no country shall frustrate that effort by the dumping of sweated goods". The implication obviously is that the offering for sale in a foreign market of goods produced under conditions which justify the name of sweating is to be described as dumping. The question immediately arises whether the term dumping should be applied to all importation of goods that have been produced by labour paid at a rate lower than the standard rates of wages in the country to which the goods are sent. The term sweating is generally taken to imply that the work is done (1) for an unduly low rate of wages, (2) with excessive hours of labour,[1] and the term dumping is evidently applied to goods so produced because it is impossible for home producers to compete on anything like equal terms. If we exclude the moral issues involved in the term sweating and think only of its economic aspects, we might well ask whether the advantages derived from a low standard of living or a greatly depreciated currency do not equally give rise to the same objection. It may be remembered in fact that during the period of German inflation objection was taken in many quarters to the so-called dumping of goods from that country.

It is evident that the intention is to apply the term in the case of what is sometimes called unfair competition, but it is very difficult to draw the line between a productive advantage which a country can enjoy without its competition being considered unfair and one against which objection can be taken. Is it a question of degree or of kind? Would the exports of Great Britain since it left the Gold Standard incur the same condemnation? The answer to the former question is pro-

[1] Fifth Report from the Select Committee of the House of Lords on the Sweating System (1890).

bably that it is a difference of kind, and to the latter "decidedly no". Hence it would seem wiser to fall back on the two definitions first given, because they at least are free from this ambiguity, and of these two, the second, that is, the Canadian, seems to be the least open to objection.

The reasons for dumping goods in a foreign country are many and various but the principal ones would seem to be

(1) The urgent necessity of obtaining abroad, as in the case of Soviet Russia, many articles required either for consumption or for industrial use for which the only means of payment is the products the country is in a position to export. This has led to the selling of such products abroad at prices far below those obtaining in Russia itself, and, it may be added, without any relation to their cost of production.

(2) The definitive policy of bringing down the price of the goods in the importing country, so as in the course of time to drive native producers out of business, and then, having captured the market, to raise the price and secure a profit that will more than compensate for earlier losses.

(3) The economic advantage to be gained by a larger scale of production. Examples have often been given, for example, with regard to Germany, that manufacturers have based their estimate of costs on the quantity absorbed by the home market, distributing all their overhead expenses over this part of their output only, and through protection have been able to keep the price at home up to this level. The additional output for the foreign market then cost them merely the outlay on raw material and labour, so that the goods could be sold at a profit in Great Britain and yet be priced well below the cost of production of British produced goods of similar make and quality.

There are some who deprecate the employment of any measures to restrain imports even though these imports may consist of dumped goods. Apart from the purely Free Trade view that imports should be encouraged because goods must be exported to pay for them, there is the argument that it is an advantage to the consumer to buy as cheaply as possible and dumped goods are in their very essence cheaper than goods otherwise obtainable. But there is another side of the question. Goods that are dumped in a country in competition with home productions tend to injure industry and to cause unemployment. Hence the advantage of cheapness may be more than counterbalanced by loss of income, and it is often urged that the justification for measures to limit or prevent dumping will be found in the fact that that method of trading so often results in economic loss to the community as a whole.

BILLS OF EXCHANGE

In International Trade payment is made for the most part by means of Bills of Exchange. A bill of exchange takes the form of an order by a manufacturer, merchant or banker to his foreign customer to pay the amount due to him to a third person at a given date which may be one, two, three or more months after the day on which the bill was drawn.

When the creditor, to use the technical term, has drawn the bill, it is passed to the debtor for acceptance, and when the bill has been duly accepted it becomes a negotiable instrument, that is to say, it confers on the holder of it a right to receive money at a given time and place which may be bought and sold. Supposing for example Messrs Brown & Jones, wool manufacturers of Leeds, have sold cloth to the value of £750 to a German importer in Berlin named Schmidt, giving him three months' credit. When the goods are dispatched it is probable that Brown & Jones will draw a bill on Schmidt for £750 ordering him to pay this amount in three months' time to their agent in Berlin—in this case we may suppose that the agent is the Deutscher Bank. If this is the case, the next step will be that Schmidt will "accept" the bill; whereupon one of two things may happen, either Brown & Jones can keep the bill in their portfolio of bills receivable and when the period of three months has expired pass it on to the Deutscher Bank for collection or, if it so happens that it is not convenient for Brown & Jones to wait so long for their money, they get their own bank in Leeds to discount it for them or in other words to buy the bill from them at a price of £750, less a deduction for interest for the unexpired portion of the three months. The bank in Leeds will in its turn pass the bill on to its Head Office in London, which again has the choice either of putting it away as a security and collecting it in Berlin when it falls due or re-discounting it with another bank.

The essence of the transaction is that Brown & Jones have parted with their goods and have received in exchange not money but the right to receive money three months hence. Everything depends therefore on the financial stability of the customer Schmidt. It may be that Brown & Jones have known him for some considerable time and have complete faith in him. Or they may have obtained a satisfactory report on his financial position from a commercial status inquiry office. In either case the credit of the German importer may be regarded as good and the exporting firm will accordingly have sufficient confidence in him to accept his signature on the bill as adequate guarantee that it will be met when due. It may, however, happen that Schmidt's signature is not considered as good enough security, and in this case Schmidt will be required either to pay cash on receipt of the invoice or to get some person or firm to guarantee payment by putting his or their name on the back of the bill or even to allow the bill to be drawn on them instead of on the importer. Institutions known as Accepting Houses exist for this purpose, and they charge a commission for the service they render.

So far it has been assumed that the exporter will draw a bill on his foreign customer. But this is not the practice followed in every case. What Brown & Jones want is that they shall receive money in exchange for their goods, and that that money shall be English money, and they are probably quite willing that Schmidt should pay them in some other way than by accepting their bill if it should be more convenient to him to do so. He may for example buy in Berlin a bill of exchange, which has been drawn by some German exporter on an English customer. This bill would carry with it the right to receive English money in London, and as Brown & Jones want English money it could very easily be arranged that they should collect what is owing to them from the English importer of German goods. This method has various advantages:

I.   Each exporter gets paid for his goods in his own currency.

II. Assuming that these two transactions are for the same amount, no money in either case will have to be sent abroad.

In practice this is the more usual method for English exporters to adopt and bills for the most part originate abroad. Various reasons may be given for this:

I.   Bills drawn abroad for goods exported to Great Britain are called Bills on London. They carry with them the right to receive payment in London, and Bills on London are as a rule in general demand.

II. The foreign exporter prefers to draw rather than to be paid by a bill drawn on a foreign centre and remitted from London, because he can get his own bill discounted for cash and it is cash he wants.

III. Moreover, the foreign importer prefers to buy bills and send them to London in payment of his debt rather than be drawn upon by the English exporter, because he hopes that in that way he may be able to gain some advantage through possible variations in the rate of exchange, and in this connection it should be borne in mind that the rate of exchange, that is, the price to be paid for each English pound, is fixed in the country in which the bill has originated and is negotiated.

It may, however, be very naturally asked: If it is an advantage to the exporter to draw a bill and for the importer to buy one and remit, how is it that English business men both exporters and importers so often let all such advantages go to the foreigner? The answer to this is that many English business men are equally well pleased with this arrangement for

(1) They are saved a certain amount of trouble;

(2) There is less risk of loss, the money by this method being collected from a firm at home whose financial stability it is much more easy to ascertain;

(3) While the foreign merchant is very frequently something of a financier and likes the chance of profit which dealing in bills affords, the English exporter more frequently confines himself to his particular line of business and prefers not to gamble in foreign exchange, with the intricacies of which he is most probably quite unfamiliar;

(4) (And this perhaps is the most important consideration of all) the English exporter can make out his invoice in pounds sterling and receive the exact sum owing to him in the same currency; there is no uncertainty as to what he will obtain from the sale of his goods.

This must not be taken to mean that bills are not drawn in England as well as abroad, but only that there are many cases in which the English exporter prefers that his foreign debtor should pay him by sending him a bill bought in that debtor's country, rather than that he should draw a bill himself, while, as already stated, the foreign exporter as a rule prefers to have it the other way.

The manner in which bills of exchange may be used to cancel mutual indebtedness between two countries without any money actually passing from the one to the other may be illustrated by the following diagram, taken from the author's *Economics of Everyday Life*:

GERMANY

```
A — — — — — sells Bill drawn on B to — — — — — D
(Creditor)                                    (Debtor)
    |           ←──────────────────            |
    |                German money              |
    | draws                                    | sends
    | Bill      - - - - - - - - - - - →         | Bill
    | on        Bill                           | to
    |           ←- - - - - - - - - - -          |
    |                English money             |
    |           ──────────────────→            |
B — — — — accepts A's Bill and pays — — — — C
(Debtor)                                   (Creditor)
```

ENGLAND

From this diagram it will be seen that *A* in Germany is selling goods to *B* in England, and at the same time *C* in England is selling goods to *D* in Germany. *A* draws a bill on *B* for the amount owing, and when it has been accepted by *B* sells the bill to *D* who owing a similar amount to *C* remits the bill to him and he collects the money from *B*. In this way both exporters receive payment for their goods in the currency of their own country, and no money has passed from one country to the other.

In connection with the passing of bills from hand to hand and treating them as negotiable instruments, reference has been made above to the buying and selling of bills, and the question naturally arises: How is the price of bills determined? This price like any other price is a matter of supply and demand. For simplicity, let us confine ourselves for the moment to bills on London, that is to say, bills drawn by foreign exporters. The supply of such bills in Paris, for example, will represent French exports to Great Britain. On the other hand the demand in Paris for such bills will represent the indebtedness of French importers for goods bought in Great Britain or, in other words, English exports to France. If there is at any time a greater supply of such bills than there is a demand for them, it would mean that, as regards Great Britain, France is exporting more than she is importing, and, as would happen in any other case where supply was in excess of demand, the price would fall. The price of what? Of bills on London, but a bill on London means the right to receive money in London, English money, and hence this over-supply in Paris of bills on London leads to a fall in value of the pound sterling. Further, as this right to receive money in London is paid for in Paris in French francs, a smaller number of French francs will suffice to purchase a given sum in pounds sterling than would have been the case if the balance of trade had been the other way. If at any time the indebtedness of England to France exactly equalled the indebtedness of France to England, we might say that the rate of exchange between the two countries would be at par. But there is no means of ascertaining at any particular moment whether such is the case, so in cases where both countries are on the Gold Standard what is called the Mint Par of Exchange is substituted for it, this Mint Par expressing the relative amounts of gold in the standard coins of the different countries. We must therefore work backwards and say that on any day when the rate of exchange between two such countries is at par it may be taken for granted that the demand for bills and the supply of bills are practically equal. It may be useful to remember that, while the United Kingdom was still on the Gold Standard, when the exchanges were at par £1 was worth 4·86⅝ dollars, 124·21 French francs, 20·43 marks, 18·159 kronor, 92·46 lire. If the daily quotations of the foreign exchanges were above these figures it was an indication that the value of the pound was above par, and if the quotations were below these figures the value of the pound was below par. The fact that gold sovereigns have not been coined and have not been in circulation since August, 1914, does not alter the fact that the standard gold sovereign does by law contain 113 grains of fine gold and is therefore equivalent to 4·86⅝ gold dollars, which would, if they could be coined, contain the same amount of fine gold. The Mint Par of Exchange then depends not on whether there are any gold sovereigns or gold pieces of twenty marks or of one dollar, or on the precise amount of gold that might at any time be contained in such coins, but on the legal requirement as to the amount of gold that each of these coins according to standard ought to contain.

It is hardly necessary to point out that since Great Britain went off the Gold Standard in September, 1931, the quotations for the pound in all gold-using countries has been very considerably below par, its precise value depending on the Demand for and the Supply of Sterling existing at the time.

THE GOLD POINTS

Between gold-using countries there are limits above and below which the rate of exchange very seldom goes. These limits are known as Specie or Gold Points. If a German importer for example had to buy American dollars[1] and he found that the rate of exchange was such that he would have to pay for them a premium amounting to more than it would cost him in freight, insurance, etc., to send gold to New York, he would naturally prefer to send the gold. Owing to there being this alternative method of payment, the rate of exchange

[1] Written while the U.S.A. were still on the Gold Standard.

between Germany and the United States of America would be kept very much within the limits above and below par set by the cost of sending gold. I am assuming for the sake of argument that no obstacle is placed by the Reichsbank or the German Government in the way of gold shipments. In theory, being on the Gold Standard implies that the notes of the country in question can be freely exchanged for gold at the Central Bank or that at any rate gold could be had for export when required. Since the Great War the financial difficulties of some countries have been such that, though nominally on the Gold Standard, the export of gold is either forbidden or greatly restricted. This being the case, rates of exchange will not infrequently be found to depart more from the par of exchange than the limits indicated by the specie points.

In the daily list of rates of exchange[1] the figures given are for what are called cheque rates, i.e. the rate at which a bill could be purchased if its face value could be obtained immediately on demand. A cheque is really nothing more nor less than a bill of exchange payable at sight. A bill, however, is only payable at some future date, generally one, two or three months after sight. Hence what the buyer of a bill actually pays is the rate of exchange of the day minus interest on the amount calculated for the duration of the bill. The rate of interest deducted, generally known as the discount rate, varies with the conditions prevailing in the Money Market at the time, one of the chief of which is the official discount rate of the Bank of England.

So far bills of exchange have been spoken of as if their only purpose was to provide a convenient way for the payment of indebtedness, arising out of the actual sale of goods. But this is not the only use to which bills of exchange may be put. Trade bills, as those which we have hitherto been discussing are generally called, are the most typical and probably the most

[1] A "List of Foreign Exchange Rates" is given on p. 219.

important form of bills of exchange, but bills can be drawn as a means of obtaining payment for a foreign debt in whatever way that debt may have arisen, or even as a means of transferring money from one country to another. Hence the supply of bills on London offered for sale in any foreign centre at any given time is likely to include bills arising out of claims to receive money in London other than those connected with the actual sale of goods. Similarly, the demand for bills on London may be taken to include the requirements of all those owing money in Great Britain, or wishing to send money to Great Britain, whether the occasion has arisen from a trade transaction or from any other form of business.

CHAPTER XIV

SOME BUSINESS INSTITUTIONS

THE ROYAL EXCHANGE

The Royal Exchange is extremely well known as a building owing to the very prominent position it occupies in the very heart of the City of London between the Mansion House on the one side and the Bank of England on the other. It is, however, much less well known as an institution. Most people, in fact, find it very difficult to say exactly what its function is.

It was first built in 1566 and opened in person by Queen Elizabeth in 1570. Some eighty houses were cleared away to make room for the new building, and the site thus obtained was presented by the City of London authorities to Sir Thomas Gresham for the erection of what was to be known as the "Burse". The building was on the model of the "Burse" at Antwerp and the name "Royal Exchange" was given to it by Queen Elizabeth on the occasion of her first visit.

SIR THOMAS GRESHAM

Sir Thomas Gresham has been described as the ablest financier of his day. During the reign of Edward VI he had been agent for the English Crown at Antwerp, then recognized as the financial centre of the world. In Elizabeth's day, however, London was rapidly coming to the front as a trading and monetary centre, the financial business of the city being transacted by the goldsmiths, who might be regarded as the bankers of that time. It is not surprising, therefore, that Sir Thomas Gresham should wish the merchants of London to have a meeting place which could rival in importance the Antwerp Burse with which during his stay in that city he had become very familiar. The need of having a place of this kind is evident when we remember that up till then the merchants and bankers used to gather in Lombard Street in the open air when they wanted to transact their business.

Gresham's building was, like many others, destroyed by the Great Fire in 1666, but it was rebuilt and a much larger building took its place. It was again destroyed in 1838, and the present building is that which then took its place. From 1774 until 1929 a portion of the building was occupied by Lloyd's, the great Marine Insurance Corporation, but that institution was removed in the latter year to the fine building in Leadenhall Street it now occupies.

Gresham's name remains with us in Gresham Street, in Gresham College, for the founding of which he left in his will the greater part of his considerable fortune, and in Gresham's Law, an oft quoted maxim in monetary theory.

The College which bears his name was to provide instruction in astronomy, geometry, physic, law, divinity, rhetoric and music, and professors were to be appointed to lecture in these various subjects.

Gresham's Law is usually stated as follows: "In a country where two kinds of money are legal tender and circulating together, the money of inferior quality will always drive out that which is better", or to put it more shortly "bad money always drives out the good".

When Elizabeth came to the throne in 1558 the coinage was in a very bad state and consequently was very injurious to both home and foreign trade. It is reported of Elizabeth's famous chancellor William Cecil, Lord Burleigh, that he laid it down as a general principle that "that realme cannot be rich whose coigne is poore or base". It is not surprising then that one of the Queen's earliest measures was the re-coinage of silver and in this work Gresham took a very prominent part. The re-coinage was a great and difficult undertaking needing both courage and statesmanship, but it was carried out with great skill and wisdom and was entirely successful.

DEALINGS IN FOREIGN CURRENCY

From its institution the Royal Exchange has always been associated with dealings in foreign currency. One of the most important matters incidental to foreign trade is the fixing of rates of exchange between the currencies of the different countries concerned. Prior to 1914 these rates were fixed at meetings of those interested in the buying or selling of foreign bills which were held in the Royal Exchange on Tuesdays and Thursdays in each week. When 'Change was over a list of prices was issued under the name of the " Course of Exchange", which was published in the various newspapers on the following day and constituted a record of currency price changes.

The following is a specimen " Course of Exchange " as it used to be issued in pre-war days:[1]

COURSE OF EXCHANGE

	Time	Prices	
Paris	short	25·24–25·29	Francs and Centimes for £1
	3 mos.	25·38–25·44	,, ,,
Brussels	,,	25·40–25·45	,, ,,
Berlin	,,	20·50–20·54	Reichsmarks and Pfennigs for £1
Amsterdam	short	12·1½–12·1¾	Guilders and Cents for £1
	3 mos.	12·2½–12·3	,, ,,
Petersburg	,,	20⅛–20¼	Pence for 1 Rouble
Stockholm	,,	18·40–18·44	Kronor and Öre for £1
Copenhagen	,,	18·39–18·43	,, ,,
Christiania	,,	18·40–18·44	,, ,,
Vienna	,,	12·05–12·10	Florins and Kreuzers for £1
Madrid	,,	43½–43¾	Pence for 1 Peso
Lisbon	,,	50–50⅛	Pence for 1 Milreis
Milan	,,	26·10–26·15	Lire and Centesimi for £1
New York	short	49⅛–49¼	Pence for 1 Dollar

By way of explanation it may be pointed out that

(1) The entries under the heading "Time" indicate when the Bill falls due, the term short being applied to short-

[1] The list of foreign centres given is somewhat abbreviated.

dated bills, i.e. to bills payable at sight (like cheques) or in anything up to ten days' time.

(2) The two prices given are for Bank Bills and Trade Bills respectively, the former, being generally discounted at a lower rate of interest, changing hands at a relatively lower price.

While Great Britain was on the Gold Standard, fluctuations in exchange rates kept, as already mentioned, within the very narrow limits known as "specie" or "gold points", but between 1914 and 1925, when Great Britain was off the Gold Standard, and again since September, 1931, fluctuations have been very much greater and consequently, instead of an official list appearing as it formerly did twice a week, we have each day in the daily newspapers a list of prices for foreign currencies which are in reality the prices at which dollars, francs, marks, lire, kronor, etc., as the case may be, have been bought or sold by the leading exchange brokers who specialize in bills of the particular country or area. Hence, the exchange lists now issued bear a fairly close resemblance to the daily lists of prices at which stocks and shares have been dealt with on the London Stock Exchange.

A list of the foreign exchange rates, as reported by the Foreign Exchange Committee under arrangement made with the London banks, appears daily in *The Times* in the form shown on the opposite page.

OTHER BUSINESS AT THE ROYAL EXCHANGE

It must not however be assumed that dealings in foreign currency was the only form of business that used to be carried on in the Royal Exchange. As already stated it was built for the merchants of the City of London to have a place in which they could transact their business, and this business was naturally of many kinds.

Not so many years ago merchants interested in the different markets could still have been seen standing about in small

List of Foreign Exchange Rates

Place		Method of quoting	Par of Exchange	April 28	April 27
New York	(3½)	\$ to £	4·86⅔	3·70–3·79	3·72–3·80
Montreal	...	\$ to £	4·86⅔	4·31–4·35	4·31–4·38
Paris	(2½)	Fr. to £	124·21	$85\frac{3}{4}$–$86\frac{11}{16}$	86¼–87½
Brussels	(3½)	Bel. to £	35·00	$24\frac{3}{16}$–$24\frac{7}{16}$	$24\frac{5}{16}$–24⅝
Milan	(4)	Lire to £	92·46	65–65⅝	65¼–66¼
Switzerland	(2)	Fr. to £	25·22	$17\frac{7}{16}$–$17\frac{11}{16}$	$17\frac{9}{16}$–$17\frac{13}{16}$
Athens	(9)	Dr. to £	375·00	580–610	580–610
Helsingfors	(6)	M. to £	193·23	225–227	225–229
Madrid	(6½)Δ	Pts. to £	25·22	39⅝–40	39⅝–40¼
Lisbon	(6½)	Escu. to £	110·00	109½–110½	109½–110½
Amsterdam	(2½)	Fl. to £	12·11	8⅜–8½	$8\frac{7}{16}$–$8\frac{9}{16}$
Berlin	(4)	M. to £	20·43	14⅝–14⅞	14¾–$15\frac{1}{16}$
Vienna	(5)	Sch. to £	34·59	31–34‡	31–34‡
Budapest	(4½)	Pen. to £	27·82	19–21*	19–21*
Prague	(3½)	Kc. to £	164·25	114–115	114–115½
Warsaw	(6)	Zloty to £	43·38	30–31	30–31
Riga	(6)	Lats to £	25·22	17–19	17–19
Bucharest	(6)	Lei to £	813·60	560–580	560–590
Constantinople	...	Pst. to £	110·00	705§	710§
Belgrade	(7½)	Din. to £	276·32	240–260	245–265
Kovno	(7)	Lit. to £	48·66	33–35	33–35
Sofia	(8½)	Lev. to £	673·66	480–520	480–520
Reval	(5½)	E.Kr. to £	18·16	12–14	12–14
Oslo	(4)	Kr. to £	18·16	19½–19⅝	19½–19⅝
Stockholm	(3½)	Kr. to £	18·16	19¼–19⅜	19¼–19⅜
Copenhagen	(3½)	Kr. to £	18·16	22⅜–22½	22⅜–22½
Alexandria	...	Pst. to £	97·50	97⅜–97⅝	97⅜–97⅝
Bombay	(3½)	Per rup.	1*s.* 6*d.*	$1/6\frac{1}{32}$–$1/6\frac{3}{32}$	1/6–1/6⅛
Calcutta	(3½)	Per rup.	1*s.* 6*d.*	$1/6\frac{1}{32}$–$1/6\frac{3}{32}$	1/6–1/6⅛
Madras	(3½)	Per rup.	1*s.* 6*d.*	$1/6\frac{1}{32}$–$1/6\frac{3}{32}$	1/6–1/6⅛
Hongkong	...	Per dol.	...	1/4½–1/5	1/4¼–1/4⅞
Kobe	(4·38)	Per yen	24·58*d.*	1/2⅞–1/3	1/2⅞–1/3⅛
Shanghai	...	Per dol.	...	1/3–1/3⅝	1/2¾–1/3½
Singapore	...	Per dol.	2*s.* 4*d.*	2/3⅝–2/3⅞	2/3⅝–2/3⅞
Batavia	(4½)	Fl. to £	12·11	8·42–8·50	8·46–8·59
Rio de Janeiro	...	Per mil.	5·90*d.*	4⅞–5⅜*d.*‡	4⅞–5⅜*d.*‡
Buenos Aires	...	Per dol.	47·62*d.*	40¾–41¾*d.**	40½–41½*d.**
Valparaiso†	...	\$ to £	40·00	Nominal	Nominal
Montevideo	...	Per dol.	4*s.* 3*d.*	32½–34½*d.*‡	Nominal
Lima†	(6½)	Soles to £	17·38	23–80	23–80
Mexico	...	Pesos to £	9·76	13·00–14·00	13·00–14·00
Manila	...	Per peso	24·66*d.*	2/7–2/8	2/7–2/8

* Official rate. † 90 days. ‡ Nominal. § Sellers.

Δ The rate for commercial bills is 6%.

Bank rates are indicated by the figures given in parentheses following the place names.

groups, settling the prices of the commodities in which they dealt, making their bargains and entering into their contracts. But as business developed and those engaged in each department of it became more numerous and more influential, one trade after another became more highly organized and erected a building of its own to serve as its headquarters.

Coal Merchants have found a home in Lower Thames Street, Corn Merchants in Mark Lane, Wool Merchants in Coleman Street, Produce Brokers in St Mary Axe, Metal Brokers in Leadenhall Street, and similar action has been taken by many other trades too numerous to mention.

At the present time, the Royal Exchange, as a place for the transaction of business, is practically deserted, its very emptiness telling the tale of the way in which London's trade has in the course of its development outgrown the accommodation provided for it in earlier days.

LLOYD'S

The name of Lloyd's is well known in every quarter of the civilized world for its connection with two very important departments of business activity, viz. the Classification of Shipping, and Insurance against risks of various kinds.

This fact, however, has led to a certain amount of confusion in the minds of people in general and it is commonly believed that the "Lloyd's" of the "Register", and the "Lloyd's" of Marine Insurance are one and the same institution. They have it is true a common origin, inasmuch as the elements of both are to be found in that Coffee House in Great Tower Street in the City of London, which was owned and run by one Edward Lloyd, but the "writing" of marine risks and the compilation of information about the ships themselves were very different functions, which tended to become more and more specialized until separate societies were formed to carry them on.

A clear distinction then should be made between

"*Lloyd's*", the Corporation whose primary object is the regulation of all matters connected with Insurance;

and "*Lloyd's Register of British and Foreign Shipping*", the Society formed for the survey and classification of vessels and the publication of a Register Book.

It is to a brief account of the former that the following pages are devoted.

THE COFFEE HOUSE

It was not till about the middle of the seventeenth century that coffee drinking became at all usual in England. Anthony à Wood, the famous Oxford antiquarian and historian, tells us that in 1656 he turned into the apothecary's near All Souls College to sample the new drink, which is described in an advertisement of the day as being "a simple Innocent thing, incomparable good for those that are troubled with melancholy".

Just about this time the first mention is made of Coffee Houses being opened in London. Ostensibly they were for the selling and drinking of coffee, but they were in addition something of the nature of our modern clubs, for they were the regular place of resort for those who had some particular interest in common, whether social, or literary, or business. There were many of these Coffee Houses in the City and in them there gathered daily people who for the most part had the same business interest. A contemporary writer refers to the Coffee Houses as being chiefly frequented by "Bankers, Stockjobbers, Frenchmen, Jews, as well as other Merchants and Gentlemen".[1]

Lloyd's Coffee House, being situated in one of the busiest trading districts and quite close to the River Thames, naturally attracted those whose business was in some way connected with shipping. It became the regular meeting place

[1] Quoted in H. G. Lay's *Marine Insurance*, a very complete history of this subject.

for shipowners, charterers, seafaring men and merchants, and as a consequence also of many who were chiefly interested in insurance against marine risks. These last were hardly as yet to be regarded as a separate section of the business community, for the "writing" of marine risks was still being undertaken by goldsmiths, merchants and others who had spare capital which they were ready to use for the insurance of ships and cargoes.

The mere fact that many of those who assembled daily at Lloyd's had a special knowledge of ships and shipping, and of sea-borne trade in general, was quite a sufficient reason for the underwriters, as they were called, also resorting there, for in their business so much depended on their obtaining the fullest possible information concerning the condition of the ships, the nature of the cargo, and the special risks connected with any particular branch of trade. Lloyd's was a regular clearing-house for all information of this kind, and Edward Lloyd made it a part of his business to collect for his patrons everything likely to be of use to them in the conduct of their business.

UNDERWRITERS

The term "underwriter", as the word suggests, was applied to those persons who signed their names at the foot of the document which insured the merchant or shipowner against the risk of loss at sea. This document came to be known as a Policy of Insurance. It was drawn up in a recognized legal form and sent round by the person who wanted to be insured to a number of those who were known to be in the habit of transacting insurance business. Anyone who agreed to take a part in the particular risk wrote his name at the foot of the policy, specifying the amount of the risk which he was willing to cover. In this way the total risk was shared by many, each one of whom could be held responsible only for that part which he had personally underwritten.

HISTORICAL OUTLINE

The earliest record of Lloyd's Coffee House, or Tavern, as it was sometimes called, is to be found in a copy of the *London Gazette* of the year 1688. It was then in Great Tower Street, but four years later the establishment was removed to a house at the corner of Lombard Street and Abchurch Lane, a situation no doubt more convenient for the more influential of the customers.

Edward Lloyd died in 1712, but already before that time marine insurance had so extended, and had become such a highly technical business, that underwriting was definitely regarded as a separate profession. The underwriters soon tended to form a kind of Regulated Company from which outsiders were jealously excluded. In 1716 they described themselves as "a number of persons each acting for himself and yet united for a common purpose". Lloyd's became the centre of their business activity and it was not long before the name became, what it has ever since remained, practically synonymous with the headquarters of Marine Insurance.

The profitable nature of the business excited the jealousy of those who wanted to have a share in it but were unable to do so, and led in the early eighteenth century to the formation of various insurance companies, some of which were altogether fraudulent in type. There was vigorous opposition on the part of Lloyd's underwriters to all projects for forming Marine Insurance Companies, but in spite of this Charters of Incorporation were in 1720 granted to two joint stock concerns, the London Assurance Corporation and the Royal Exchange Assurance Corporation, and for more than a century these two companies together with the Society of Lloyd's underwriters, which we may now speak of simply as Lloyd's, shared a complete monopoly of the Marine Insurance business. This monopoly came to an end in 1824, and since that date many other companies have been formed to under-take the same class of business.

The Coffee House in Abchurch Lane continued to flourish in very much its original form until 1770, when that section of the regular customers which confined its activities to Marine Insurance decided to establish itself in quarters of its own. The underwriters found temporary accommodation in Pope's Head Alley, but in 1774 they transferred themselves to the Royal Exchange, which remained their permanent home till they removed in 1929 to a new building of their own in Leadenhall Street. In the "New Lloyd's" established in the Royal Exchange the underwriters still preserved the old Coffee House idea and the old historic name, but they devoted their energies to the business of Marine Insurance and ap-pointed a "master" to look after the catering arrangements.

One of the most important events in the history of Lloyd's occurred in 1871 when the society was granted a Charter of Incorporation, bestowing upon it the privileges of a Corpora-tion for the purpose of the following three objects:[1]

(1) The carrying on of the business of Marine Insurance *by members of the Society*.

(2) The protection of the interests of the members of the Society in respect of shipping, cargoes and freight.

(3) The collection, publication and diffusion of intelligence and information relating to shipping.

The desire to bring other forms of insurance within the scope of the Corporation's activity led to a demand for the amendment of the Charter and this result was accomplished in 1911, the objects of the Corporation being then so stated as to cover the business of insurance of every description.

This must not be taken to mean that Lloyd's underwriters now undertook these other classes of business for the first time. As individuals many of them had previously for quite

[1] H. G. Lay, *Marine Insurance*.

a long time insured all kinds of risks, but it was only in 1911 that as a Corporation Lloyd's was in a position to control these additional activities of its members.

LLOYD'S LIST

The third of the objects mentioned above has to do with shipping intelligence. Reference has already been made to the fact that Edward Lloyd was in the habit of providing his patrons with all sorts of miscellaneous information about ships and shipping. For a time he embodied this in a kind of written news-sheet, but in 1696 he began the publication three times a week of a printed sheet which he called *Lloyd's News*. After about six months this was discontinued and he reverted to the old written form.

Lloyd's List which was first published in 1726 was quite distinct from *Lloyd's News*, but it may be said to have carried on the tradition of its predecessor. *Lloyd's List* can best be described as a daily newspaper devoted to the interests of the shipping, commercial and marine insurance sections of the business community. It has had an unbroken record from 1726 to the present day and hence can claim to be the second oldest newspaper in existence, the *London Gazette*, the oldest, having preceded it by some sixty years.

When in 1770 the underwriters broke away from the rather miscellaneous crowd which gathered at the Coffee House in Abchurch Lane, and found new quarters for themselves in Pope's Head Alley, they acquired the property in *Lloyd's List* and its publication is still one of the many activities of Lloyd's.

The collecting of the information published in *Lloyd's List*, as well as of that communicated to members in various other ways, has necessitated the creation of an immense intelligence organization with outposts all over the world.

The system includes

    (1) *Lloyd's Agents*, established in every port to furnish information about shipping casualties, etc., to render

assistance when needed, and to protect the interests of underwriters generally.

(2) *Lloyd's Signal Stations*, erected on prominent positions along the coast of this and other countries to report the movements of ships and to transmit messages between owners and captains.

Through these and other channels of communication the most accurate and up-to-date information is obtained of all matters pertaining to shipping in any part of the world and is made available by Lloyd's for the service of all concerned or in any way interested.

INSURING AT LLOYD'S

A few words must be added about the way insurance at Lloyd's is effected and the measures that are taken by the Corporation to protect the interests of those who are insured.

When anyone wishes to take out an insurance at Lloyd's of any particular nature he does not himself go to the individual underwriters and ask them to undertake the risk, but he goes to a Lloyd's broker, an insurance specialist, who places the risk for him with a group of underwriters each of whom becomes personally liable to the assured for such portion of the risk as he has underwritten. The broker receives the premium and distributes it amongst the underwriters, and in case of loss he collects from them their respective shares of it.

To become an underwriting member of Lloyd's is by no means a simple thing. There is the most careful scrutiny of the applicant's financial and general standing, and he is required to deposit with the Committee securities to an amount of not less than £5000 in value. He has, moreover, to pass each year the "audit" not only of his underwriting accounts but also of his financial position generally. This is conducted under the Committee's direct supervision and is of a very drastic character. In this way insurers have the security that those who undertake the risks have the means of meeting all legitimate claims which may be made against them.

THE STOCK EXCHANGE

HISTORICAL OUTLINE

The London Stock Exchange as an Institution may be said to date from 1773, when the dealers in stocks and shares who resorted to New Jonathan's Coffee House in 'Change Alley decided that the place should be called "The Stock Exchange" and had the name written up over the door.

Already in the last quarter of the seventeenth century and more especially after 1694 when the Bank of England, the first Joint Stock Bank, received its charter, dealing in stocks and shares had become quite a recognized occupation.

It was about the year 1688 (says Lord Macaulay) that the word stockjobber was first heard in London. In the short space of four years a crowd of companies, every one of which confidently held out to subscribers the hope of immense gains, sprang into existence. Some of these companies took large mansions and printed their advertisements in gilded letters. Others, less ostentatious, were content with ink, and met at coffee-houses in the neighbourhood of the Royal Exchange. Jonathan's and Garraway's were in a constant ferment with brokers, buyers, sellers, meetings of directors, meetings of proprietors.[1]

This extract serves to remind us of the rage for speculation which began about that time. The public rushed to subscribe the capital for the new companies and the shares were freely bought and sold. Dealings were by no means confined to the Coffee Houses mentioned; the "jobbers", as the dealers in stocks and shares were called, carried on their business in any convenient place, such as the Royal Exchange, the Rotunda of the Bank of England, and even the streets near the Royal

---

[1] Macaulay, *History of England*, Chap. XIX.

Exchange, especially Cornhill and Lombard Street and the Alleys connecting them, 'Change Alley and Sweeting's Alley.

The Coffee House most frequented by the stock and share dealers was undoubtedly Old Jonathan's in 'Change Alley, and this in the early eighteenth century came to be regarded as their headquarters. When this house was burnt down in 1748, the New Jonathan's erected on the same site took its place, and this, as stated above, adopted in 1773 the name of the Stock Exchange.

It was about this time, too, that there developed a tendency to specialize in the different kinds of securities, and this led to business in the public funds being transacted at the Bank of England, in foreign securities at the Royal Exchange, and in other stocks and shares at the newly established Stock Exchange at New Jonathan's.

By the end of the century, the membership of the Stock Exchange had so increased that New Jonathan's did not provide sufficient accommodation for the transaction of business and it was resolved to build a larger and more convenient house. A site was obtained at the farther end of Capel Court, an opening out of Bartholomew Lane, and to the new building erected on it the Stock Exchange was transferred in 1802. It has been rebuilt since then but it still occupies the same site, well secluded from the public view.

CONSTITUTION

The move to Capel Court coincided with a new departure in the constitution of the Stock Exchange, for it was then formed into a Joint Stock Company. The London Stock Exchange has therefore like Lloyd's a kind of dual existence, for it is on the one hand a company making profits out of which it pays dividends to its shareholders, and on the other it is an institution which regulates the dealing in stocks and shares, which prescribes the conditions of membership, and which lays down rules which all members have to observe.

Shareholders must be members but all members are not necessarily shareholders, though under present conditions all new members are required to take up at least one share. The administration is carried on by two elected bodies, known respectively as the "Managers" and the "Committee". The former, being more of the nature of a Board of Directors, may be regarded as looking after the interests of the shareholders; the latter is the real management, for it regulates and controls the working of the Stock Exchange as a public institution, sees that the rules are observed by its members and acts as a court of arbitration in all cases of dispute.

BROKERS AND JOBBERS

Members are of two classes—Brokers and Jobbers—and here again we may institute a comparison with Lloyd's, for stockbrokers, like Lloyd's brokers, transact business on behalf of their clients, while jobbers, like underwriters, have all their dealings with the brokers. Thus the public have no direct contact with the actual dealers in the shares; they place their orders with a stockbroker who, acting on their behalf, goes to a jobber who specializes in the particular class of share and gets a price from him. On the floor of the "House", as the Stock Exchange is called, are to be found separate groups of jobbers, forming the markets for the different classes of securities. Thus a broker wanting to sell railway stock for one of his clients knows exactly where to go in order to find a jobber prepared to buy or to sell that stock as the case may be. He asks for a price and gets a double quotation such as may be seen in the daily list of Stock Exchange prices, say $95\frac{3}{8}$–$\frac{5}{8}$. This means that the jobber is a buyer at $95\frac{3}{8}$ and a seller at $95\frac{5}{8}$. The difference between these prices is what is known as the "jobber's turn".

STOCKS AND SHARES

The phrase "stocks and shares" is in such common use that there is some danger of forgetting that the two terms are not so inseparable as they appear, but that they are in fact the names of two easily distinguishable classes of security. Reference was made in Chapter IV to Adam Smith's use of the term "stock" in connection with the capital of a business or company. Stocks, using the word in the plural, would with him generally mean a number of such capitals taken together. The current use is rather more specialized and more restricted. If, for example, one speaks of buying Great Western Railway stock, one means buying a form of security which represents the ownership of a certain amount of the capital of that Railway Company, and the general term for transactions of that kind would be "buying stocks". Of some companies the capital is divided up into portions of a fixed amount, in this case we speak of the portions of capital as shares. Thus a company might have a capital of £100,000 divided into 100,000 shares of £1 each. This is a very convenient method, because it enables the small investor to acquire such portion of the capital of an undertaking as his means will allow. In the case of stocks the capital is not so subdivided, though it is very usual for dealings in it to be in units of £100. One could, however, for example, buy an odd amount such as £2541 of a certain stock, obtaining for one's money a corresponding portion of the nominal capital of the company. The difference between stocks and shares, then, is that when buying shares you buy a certain number of units of the capital, each £1, £5, £50, or even 1s. or 5s. as the case might be, but when buying stocks you buy a certain portion of the capital not divided up in this way. Stocks are quoted on the Stock Exchange at so much per £100 of stock, shares at so much per share, the price paid varying with the market conditions of the day.

THE ACCOUNT

With the exception of certain classes of securities which have to be paid for in cash, Stock Exchange transactions are as a rule settled on the next Account Day. There are two accounts in each month, one about the middle and the other towards the end. Before the war the first day of each account was called "contango" day and on this day arrangements could be made if desired for carrying over the transaction to the next account. This practice, however, is now prohibited and all transactions must be completed within the account. This regulation has very much restricted the operations of what are called the Bulls and the Bears and so has tended to put a check on mere speculation. The Bulls are persons who buy stock without intending to pay for it, calculating on a rise in price which would enable them to sell before payment has to be made, in which case all they would have to do is to collect the profit. The Bears, on the other hand, are persons who sell what they have not got in the expectation that the price will fall and that they will be able to buy cheaper before they have to deliver the "scrip".

DEFAULT

Every stockbroker has a personal responsibility for the bargains he makes on behalf of his clients. He buys, for example, on the instructions of a client a large parcel of stock. The client, perhaps, intended it merely as a speculation and calculated on an improvement in the market which would enable him to sell again before he had to pay for it. His calculation went wrong—the price fell, and there was a heavy loss. If he then failed to pay for the stock, the stockbroker would be obliged to bear the loss himself. Many such experiences might bring him to ruin and if he failed to meet his obligations at any account he would be declared a defaulter. The failure of a member of the Stock Exchange leads to his being "hammered". One of the waiters goes up into the rostrum, gives three strokes with a mallet, and then announces "Mr X has not complied with his bargains". The Stock Exchange has the reputation of being a rather boisterous assembly, and it has been said that it is only on occasions of this kind that the "House" becomes really quiet and serious, though doubtless this statement must not be taken too literally.

The fact that some people use the Stock Exchange very largely as a means of speculating, not to say gambling, in stocks and shares should not be allowed to obscure the very important part it plays in the economic life of the country. The accumulation of fresh capital which is so essential to the development of business enterprise is in the first instance stimulated by opportunities for remunerative investment, but it is also and still further stimulated by the knowledge that through the Stock Exchange investments that have been made can be unmade. Stocks and shares that have been bought can be sold at any time and the money so released can be applied to the purchase of other securities or can be used to meet some particular need that may have arisen. It is by providing a means of investing, transferring or realizing capital as and when desired that this institution renders its chief service to the community as a whole.

INDEX

INDEX

Printed in the United States
By Bookmasters